Bloom's
GUIDES

Emily Brontë's
Wuthering Heights

The Adventures of Huckleberry Finn

All the Pretty Horses

Animal Farm

The Autobiography of Malcolm X

The Awakening

Beloved

Beowulf

Brave New World

The Canterbury Tales

The Catcher in the Rye

The Chosen

The Crucible

Cry, the Beloved Country

Death of a Salesman

Fahrenheit 451

Frankenstein

The Glass Menagerie

The Grapes of Wrath

Great Expectations

The Great Gatsby

Hamlet

The Handmaid's Tale

The House on Mango Street

I Know Why the Caged Bird Sings

The Iliad

Invisible Man

Jane Eyre

Lord of the Flies

Macbeth

Maggie: A Girl of the Streets

The Member of the Wedding

The Metamorphosis

Native Son

1984

The Odyssey

Oedipus Rex

Of Mice and Men

One Hundred Years of Solitude

Pride and Prejudice

Ragtime

The Red Badge of Courage

Romeo and Juliet

The Scarlet Letter

A Separate Peace

Slaughterhouse-Five

Snow Falling on Cedars

The Stranger

A Streetcar Named Desire

The Sun Also Rises

A Tale of Two Cities

The Things They Carried

To Kill a Mockingbird

Uncle Tom's Cabin

The Waste Land

Wuthering Heights

Bloom's
GUIDES

Emily Brontë's
Wuthering Heights

Edited & with an Introduction
by Harold Bloom

BLOOM'S
LITERARY CRITICISM
An imprint of Infobase Publishing

Bloom's Guides: Wuthering Heights

Copyright © 2008 by Infobase Publishing

Introduction © 2008 by Harold Bloom

All rights reserved. No part of this book may be reproduced or utilized in any form or by any means, electronic or mechanical, including photocopying, recording, or by any information storage or retrieval systems, without permission in writing from the publisher. For information contact:

Bloom's Literary Criticism
An imprint of Infobase Publishing
132 West 31st Street
New York, NY 10001

Library of Congress Cataloging-in-Publication Data
Emily Brontë's Wuthering Heights / [edited and with introduction by] Harold Bloom.
    p. cm. — (Bloom's guides)
  Includes bibliographical references and index.
  ISBN 978-0-7910-9831-8 (hardcover)
  1. Brontë, Emily, 1818–1848. Wuthering Heights. I. Bloom, Harold. II. Title: Wuthering Heights.

  PR4172.W73E453 2008
  823'.8—dc22
                            2007048752

Bloom's Literary Criticism books are available at special discounts when purchased in bulk quantities for businesses, associations, institutions, or sales promotions. Please call our Special Sales Department in New York at (212) 967-8800 or (800) 322-8755.

You can find Bloom's Literary Criticism on the World Wide Web at
http://www.chelseahouse.com

Contributing Editor: Janyce Marson
Cover design by Takeshi Takahashi
Printed in the United States of America
Bang EJB 10 9 8 7 6 5 4 3 2 1
This book is printed on acid-free paper.

All links and Web addresses were checked and verified to be correct at the time of publication. Because of the dynamic nature of the Web, some addresses and links may have changed since publication and may no longer be valid.

Contents

Introduction

HAROLD BLOOM

Wuthering Heights is one of those canonical works or classics that reward readers at every level of literary sophistication. I suspect that this has to do with the strangeness or originality that Emily Brontë's idiosyncratic "northern romance" possesses in such abundance. *Wuthering Heights* is like nothing else in the language, though the closest work to it, the sister-book as it were, is Charlotte Brontë's *Jane Eyre*. Yet Charlotte rejected the affinity and regarded Heathcliff as "a mere demon." Heathcliff is much more than that; as a negative hero or hero-villain he has the sublimity of Captain Ahab in Herman Melville's *Moby-Dick* and something even of the darkened splendor of Satan in Milton's *Paradise Lost*. Emily Brontë's implicit model for Heathcliff was the long poem *Manfred*, a self-portrait by Lord Byron in which the Romantic poet allows himself to absorb aspects of Milton's Satan. Despite Heathcliff's sadism, he is however satanic primarily in his wounded pride. His obsessive love for Catherine Earnshaw is the only principle of his being. This passion is so monumental and so destructive, of everyone, that it seems inadequate and imprecise to call it "love." To define the mutual attachment between Heathcliff and the first Catherine is a difficult enterprise but is essential to understanding *Wuthering Heights*.

One hesitates to term the relationship between Heathcliff and Catherine even potentially sexual, since sexual love unites in act, but not in essence, and Catherine is capable of saying: "I am Heathcliff." As you reread *Wuthering Heights*, you come to see that there are two orders of reality in the novel, with only tenuous connectors between them. One is *both* social and natural, while the other is neither, being the realm of dreams, ghosts, visions, and (most importantly) the transcendental yearnings of all our childhoods. That second realm is neither psychological nor spiritual; Emily Brontë was neither a moral psychologist nor a Christian, though she was a clergyman's daughter. Doomed, like all her siblings, to an early death from tuberculosis, she learned to dwell in her deepest self, which is the theater where the drama of *Wuthering Heights* is performed. The two oldest Brontë sisters, Maria and Elizabeth, died in 1825, aged eleven and ten. Charlotte, the family survivor, died at thirty-eight, after mourning the deaths of Emily, aged thirty, her brother Branwell, at thirty-one, and Anne, at twenty-nine. *Wuthering Heights*, completed when Emily Brontë was twenty-eight, gives us a world in which everyone marries young because they seem to know that they will not live very long. Catherine Earnshaw dies at eighteen, Hindley at twenty-seven, Isabella at thirty-one, Linton Heathcliff at seventeen, Edgar at thirty-nine, and Heathcliff, probably, at about thirty-seven. At the end of the book, Hareton and the second Catherine are twenty-four and eighteen, respectively, when they happily marry. While the urgency of all this has both its societal and its natural aspects, the larger suggestion is a kind of doom-eagerness, impatient alike of society and of nature.

Moral judgments, whether of her own day or of ours, become rapidly irrelevant in the world of Emily Brontë's one novel. Though the book portrays both social and natural energies, these are dwarfed by the preternatural energies of Heathcliff and of the antithetical side of the first Catherine. Where daemonic energy so far exceeds ours, then daemonic suffering will also be present, perhaps also in excess of our own. But such suffering is foreign to us; Emily Brontë accepts the aesthetic risk of endowing Heathcliff with very little pathos recognizable by us. We wonder at his terrible sufferings, as he slowly dies from lack of sleep and lack of food, but we do not *feel* his agony, because he has become even more distant from us. We are partly moved by the first Catherine's death, since both society and nature are involved in her decline, but partly we stand away from participation, because Catherine is also very much of the realm she shares with Heathcliff. For the last half-year of his life, she is a ghostly presence, but one not much different from what she has been for him before.

The first Catherine is the only bridge we have to the mystery of Heathcliff, since only Catherine lives both in the realistic and occult worlds that confront one another in *Wuthering Heights*. E.M. Forster, in his *Aspects of the Novel* (1927), remarked that: "*Wuthering Heights* has no mythology beyond what these two characters provide: no great book is more cut off from the universals of Heaven and Hell." That seems true to me, and it makes Emily Brontë's great narrative an anomaly; it is of no clear genre. But it gives us, finally, something larger and stronger even than Heathcliff, something that I would want to call more than the personal vision of Emily Brontë. The transcendental element in the book cannot be assigned any traditional name, but its force and its persuasiveness cannot be evaded or ignored. Emily Brontë prophesied no religion except that of the "God within my breast," and *Wuthering Heights* profoundly implies that Heathcliff and Catherine reunite in a here and now that yet is not our present world or any world to come for most among us.

Biographical Sketch

Emily Jane Brontë was born on July 30, 1818, at Thornton, near Bradford, Yorkshire. She was the fifth child and fourth daughter of the Reverend Patrick Brontë and Maria Branwell (Patrick later changed his name to Branwell Brontë). Emily's sisters Charlotte (1816–1855) and Anne (1820–1849) were also writers, as was her brother, Branwell (1817–1848), to a more limited extent. In 1820 the family moved to Haworth, where Branwell senior obtained a curacy. The next year Emily's mother died; her sister Elizabeth kept house for the family until she herself died in 1842. Emily briefly attended the Clergy Daughters' School at Cowan Bridge in 1824–25 but thereafter was largely educated at home. Beginning in 1826 the Brontë children, fascinated by some toy soldiers their father had brought home, conceived of an imaginary African kingdom called Angria; later Emily and Anne invented a separate kingdom in the Pacific called Gondal. They all wrote poems and prose sketches about these kingdoms for the rest of their lives.

For a period in 1835 Emily accompanied Charlotte as a tutor at a school in East Yorkshire, but she was unhappy there and quickly returned to Haworth. In 1837 or 1838 she worked as a governess at Law Hill, near Halifax; a house near this school, High Sunderland Hall, is thought by some scholars to be the chief inspiration for Wuthering Heights. In 1842, as part of a plan to open a school at Haworth, Emily went to the Pensionnat Heger in Brussels with Charlotte to study languages; but, although she was praised for her intellect and especially her mastery of French, her forbidding manner attracted few pupils.

Returning to Haworth late in 1842, Emily devoted herself to the writing of poetry about Gondal. Much of this poetry is full of the same violent, cruel characters that populate *Wuthering Heights*. In the autumn of 1845 Charlotte discovered a notebook containing this poetry; although Emily was at first highly incensed at the discovery, she was gradually persuaded to let Charlotte seek its publication. In 1846 a collection of verse by Charlotte, Emily, and Anne appeared as *Poems by Currer, Ellis, and Acton Bell* (their respective pseudonyms). Emily wrote only one more poem in her lifetime, for by this time she was at work on her one novel.

Wuthering Heights was written between October 1845 and June 1846 and published in December 1847, again under the pseudonym of Ellis Bell. It was not well received and puzzled most of its readers; many of them regarded it as excessively morbid, violent, and indelicate. In the years since Emily Brontë's death, the book has found its readership and a steadily growing reputation. It is now considered one of the masterpieces of nineteenth-century fiction and one of the most original novels in English literature.

It is conjectured that Emily was working on an expanded version of *Wuthering Heights* in the final year or so before her death; but this version, if there was one, has not been found. Otherwise, little is known of the final two years of her life. Emily Brontë died of tuberculosis at the age of thirty on December 19, 1848.

The Story Behind the Story

The history of the first publication and early reception of *Wuthering Heights* is as tumultuous and fraught with speculation as the events depicted in the novel. Sometime in July 1847 *Wuthering Heights* and *Agnes Grey* (the latter by Emily's sister Anne) were sent to an obscure British publisher, Thomas Cautley Newby, under the name of Ellis (Emily) and Acton (Anne) Bell. Newby wrote back to Currer Bell (Charlotte Brontë) that he would accept the manuscripts of Ellis and Acton Bell on the condition that they would agree to share in the costs of production. Left with no other offers, the sisters agreed to this financial arrangement on July 15 of that year. The agreement was that the sisters would advance Newby 50 pounds and, upon the sale of the first 250 copies, he would refund them the same. However, Newby, a newly established publisher and printer who avidly sought unknown writers, proved himself unscrupulous and fraudulent. He never refunded the Brontë sisters the money rightfully due to them. Even more egregious is that though Emily and Anne had made corrections to the first proof sheets, which they received in August, Newby consistently ignored their letters and, instead, delayed publication until after Charlotte's *Jane Eyre*, published on October 16, 1847, proved to be successful. Once the disreputable Newby realized that he could capitalize on the name of Bell, he proceeded to publish their novels, albeit without having made the corrections they had submitted and actually published fewer than the previously agreed upon number of copies. Even the appearance of Newby's first edition was disappointing as there were two different bindings, a ribbed deep claret for private purchasers and a plain cloth one for privately funded circulating libraries such as Mudie's* of Oxford Street and W.H. Smith and Son, Strand, which influenced Victorian literature. Though Charlotte would later try to convince Emily that Newby was corrupt, Emily remained misguidedly loyal to him, refusing to exchange him for Charlotte's far more reputable publisher, Smith, Elder & Company.

In addition to his breach of the financial contract with Emily and Anne Brontë, Newby's deceptive practices extended to his need to conceal the true identity of Ellis (and Acton) Bell so as to exploit the initial confusion for his own financial gain. In his unbridled greed, Newby went as far as purchasing newspaper advertisements that implied that the three sisters were the same person. This confusion was echoed in the earliest reviews of *Wuthering Heights*. *The Athenaeum*, in its July 8, 1848, review, surmised that all three novels (*Jane Eyre*, *Wuthering Heights*, and *Agnes Grey*) were possibly the work of the same author while punning on their *nom de guerre*:

> The three Bells, as we took occasion to observe when reviewing *Wuthering Heights*, ring in a chime so harmonious as to prove that they have issued from the same mould. The resemblance borne by their novels to each other is curious. . . . The Bells must be warned against their fancy for dwelling upon what is disagreeable. . . . Were the metal of this Bell foundry of baser quality that it is, it would be lost time to point out flaws and take exceptions. As matters stand, our hints may not be without their use to future 'castings.'

Two years following Emily Brontë's death, Sydney Dobell, in an article published in *The Palladium*, opined that *Wuthering Heights* was the early work of Currer Bell, the female author of *Jane Eyre*, characterizing the book as masculine and finding cause to praise certain elements.

> Who is Currer Bell? is a question which has been variously answered, and has lately, we believe, received in well-informed quarters, a satisfactory reply. A year or two ago, we mentally solved the problem thus: Currer Bell is a woman. Every word she utters is female. Not feminine, but female. There is a sex about it which cannot be mistaken, even in its manliest attire. Though she translated the manuscript of angels—every thought neutral and every feeling cryptogamous—her *voice* would betray her.

* * * *

Laying aside Wildfell Hall, we open *Wuthering Heights*, as at once the earlier in date and ruder in execution. We look upon it as the flight of an impatient fancy fluttering in the very exultation of young wings; sometimes beating against its solitary bars, but turning, rather to exhaust, in a circumscribed space, the energy and agility which it may not yet spend in the heavens—a youthful story, written for oneself in solitude, and thrown aside till other successes recall the eyes to it in hope.

* * * *

. . . [T]here are passages in this book of *Wuthering Heights* of which any novelist, past or present, might be proud. . . . There are few things in modern prose to surpass these pages for native power. We cannot praise too warmly the brave simplicity, the unaffected air of intense belief . . . the nice provision of the possible even in the highest effects of the supernatural. . . .

When Newby brazenly submitted Anne's second novel, *The Tenant of Wildfell Hall*, as the work of Currer Bell to the American publishing house Harper Brothers, Charlotte and Anne went to London in summer 1848 to meet with Smith, Elder and confirm that the Bells were, in fact, three sisters.** When Newby died in 1882, his name and notoriety were added to a long list of opportunistic publishers before him, though he managed, unbeknownst to him, to have delivered an abiding literary classic that he could never appreciate. Ironically, his disreputable and underhanded participation in publishing *Wuthering Heights* served to augment the novel's mystique.

Significantly, it was Sydney Dobell's review in *The Palladium*, shortly before a second edition appeared, that gave Charlotte confidence that *Wuthering Heights* would now receive a more favorable reception. It should be noted, however, that Dobell's review was not entirely complimentary. As Melvin Watson points out ("*Wuthering Heights* and the Critics"), though Dobell "expiated on the brilliance of the work more fully than had anyone else, . . . he makes the gross error of failing to perceive that it is the mature work of a sensitive artist." In 1850, on the occasion of the issuing of the second edition of *Wuthering Heights*, Charlotte made a final attempt to persuade the readership that the Bells were three separate writers by relating the circumstances in which they originally decided upon the *nom de guerre* of Bell.

> We had very early cherished the dream of one day becoming authors. . . . We agreed to arrange a small selection of our poems, and, if possible, get them printed. Averse to personal publicity, we veiled our own names under Currer, Ellis and Acton Bell; the ambiguous choice being dictated by a sort of conscientious scruple at assuming Christian names, positively masculine, while we did not like to declare ourselves women, because— without at that time suspecting that our mode of writing and thinking was not what is called "feminine"—we had a vague impression that authoresses are liable to be looked on with prejudice; we had noticed how critics sometimes use for their chastisement the weapon of personality, and for their reward, a flattery, which is not true praise.

Having explained the reasons for their assumed literary identities, the remainder of her biographical sketch in the new edition of *Wuthering Heights* is a eulogy to Emily Brontë's abundant imagination and absolute determination to remain independent: "Under an unsophisticated culture, inartificial tastes, and an unpretending outside, lay a secret power and fire that might have informed the brain and kindled the veins of a hero; but she had no worldly wisdom . . . she would fail to defend her most manifest rights, to consult her most legitimate advantage." With Charlotte having settled the issue of true identity and unequivocally set forth all the personal attributes that she admired in her beloved sister, it would not be until the second decade of the twentieth century that Emily Brontë would be appreciated and acknowledged for what she achieved in *Wuthering Heights*.

Notes

*In 1842 Charles Edward Mudie established "Mudie's Select" library where, for various sums, subscribers could borrow one or more books at a time. Mudie proved to be an influential entrepreneur and was therefore instrumental in making available novels and other works of fiction to his members. Since he also advertised a list of "principal New and Choice Books" he intended to stock, he also became an unwitting publicist. Eventually, the advent of public libraries during the nineteenth century weakened these private establishments.

**Newby's shameful career lasted until 1874, at which time his publishing house ceased operations. Indeed, in that very same year in which he published *Wuthering Heights*, Newby also published Anthony Trollope's first novel, *The Macdermots of Ballycloran*, attributing it to Trollop's mother, Frances, already a successful novelist, as a means to exploit the family name for his own financial gain.

List of Characters

Catherine (Cathy) Earnshaw is the beautiful, passionate, and destructive heroine of *Wuthering Heights*. She finds her soul mate in the dark, brooding Heathcliff but marries a much weaker man and destroys their happiness. She has grown up with Heathcliff, an adopted gypsy child, and their friendship strengthens during an orphaned adolescence under the tyrannical rule of her older brother. Defiant, domineering, and impetuous, Cathy finds a new admirer in the delicate, pampered Edgar Linton, but she grows delirious with grief when a spurned Heathcliff leaves the Heights. Her joy at his return, a year into her marriage to Edgar, is so great that her husband's jealousy is aroused. Violent arguments ensue, and Cathy self-destructively hastens her own end through rage and starvation. She dies in childbirth. Her spirit literally and figuratively haunts the rest of the novel. Heathcliff is tortured by her memory, farmers claim to see her ghost walking the moors, and the narrator himself encounters her frightening dream-figure. Cathy's tragedy also threatens until the last to haunt and repeat itself in the life of her daughter.

Heathcliff is the passionate, vengeful hero of Brontë's novel. His mysterious origin makes him a social outcast among the landed gentry, and his destitute adolescence creates a stoical, calculating temperament. He is Cathy's physical and spiritual equal, but when she accepts Edgar's attentions, he deserts the Heights. He returns mysteriously rich and educated, destroying the equilibrium of Cathy's marriage. He elopes with Isabella Linton to destroy her brother, Edgar, and lures Hindley Earnshaw into gambling away his rights to Wuthering Heights. Heathcliff's thirst for revenge is only checked when he senses the imminence of his own death and, with it, a final reunion with his ghostly beloved.

Nelly Dean is the housekeeper whose account of the events at Wuthering Heights comprises the body of the narrator's—Mr.

Lockwood's—records. She is a sturdy local woman whose common-sensical nature contrasts sharply with the unfettered passions of her subjects. Having grown up in the Earnshaw household and served as Cathy's maid during her marriage, Nelly has a privileged vantage point. She is a keen and critical observer who is not above listening at doors or reading letters. After Cathy's death, Nelly becomes the nursemaid of her daughter, Catherine, and witnesses the twists of fortune of her new charge. She also witnesses Heathcliff's strange and ghostly death, which contradicts her own rational worldview.

Mr. Lockwood is the secondhand narrator of *Wuthering Heights*. The novel consists of his diary entries during a period as Heathcliff's tenant and records the story he hears from Nelly. Lockwood is a young London gentleman who rents the old Linton estate from Heathcliff and soon grows curious about his misanthropic landlord with the beautiful widowed daughter-in-law. Lockwood is little more than a passive listener, confined to his bed with a cold for most of the novel, yet his impartial facade unsuccessfully hides his admiration for the second Catherine Linton.

Edgar Linton is Cathy's husband. He is a soft, effeminate character completely in the power of his willful, temperamental wife. He suffers through her rages and illnesses, and when she dies he resigns himself to an isolated life devoted to his daughter. His gentle, timorous nature contrasts entirely with vengeful Heathcliff's passion. His rival destroys his happiness a second time by kidnapping his adolescent daughter, Catherine. The blow is so devastating that Edgar soon dies of grief.

Isabella Linton is Edgar's younger sister. She is a pampered child and a selfish, reckless young woman. When Heathcliff returns, Isabella falls in love with him and they elope, despite her brother's prohibitions and Cathy's serious illness. She is shocked by Heathcliff's cruelty but counters with her own viciousness and flees the Heights on the night of Cathy's funeral, when Heathcliff is overcome by grief. Here she exits the story, moving to the south, giving birth to a son, and then dying twelve years later.

Hindley Earnshaw is Cathy's older brother and Heathcliff's hated enemy. He is jealous of Heathcliff as a child and tries to ruin him once he becomes master of Wuthering Heights. He reduces Heathcliff to abject poverty but falls into bad ways himself after his wife dies. When Heathcliff returns a rich gentleman after several years' absence, Hindley takes him in as a boarder to satiate his greed for gambling. He soon loses his entire estate at cards. Until his death Hindley leads a violent, drunken existence indebted to his enemy.

Catherine Linton is Cathy's daughter and the heroine of the second half of the novel. She has both Edgar's gentleness, playing the devoted daughter during an idyllic childhood, and Cathy's willful haughtiness, which manifests itself during her enforced residence at the Heights. Heathcliff kidnaps her and forces her when she is sixteen to marry his dying son, Linton. She is soon widowed, orphaned, and stripped of her inheritance, and her miserable life at the Heights begins to parallel that of her mother's under a tyrannical brother. The love she eventually discovers for her rough, illiterate cousin Hareton nonetheless leads to a brighter future.

Hareton Earnshaw is the son of Hindley, Cathy's older brother. When his mother dies soon after his birth, his father becomes a violent drunkard. Hareton grows up angry and unloved. Clear parallels are drawn between the downtrodden Hareton and the sullen young Heathcliff. Hareton's life threatens to end tragically when the beautiful Catherine Linton arrives at the Heights and scorns her cousin's gestures of friendship. She eventually overcomes her prejudices and Heathcliff dies before he can destroy a union that returns Wuthering Heights to its rightful heir and matches the second generation's true hero and heroine.

Linton Heathcliff is Heathcliff's sickly son, the product of the unhappy union of Heathcliff and Isabella Linton. Raised for his first twelve years by his mother, he is taken to the Heights after her death. Linton is small-minded and cruel despite his physical weaknesses. Terrified of his father and acting only out of self-preservation, he helps Heathcliff kidnap Catherine and marries her against her will. Linton soon dies, having impressed the reader with his petty selfishness, which stands in sharp contrast to Hareton's rough but well-meaning generosity.

Summary and Analysis

Emily Brontë's *Wuthering Heights* is a love story set in the desolate moorlands of northern England at the end of the eighteenth century. It spans a period of some forty years, following the repercussions of the fiery, doomed love of the novel's protagonists, Cathy and Heathcliff. Passion, both love and hatred, erupt with ferocity in Brontë's Gothic world, yet she simultaneously creates a degree of critical distance from the drama by using a disinterested secondhand narrator. Lockwood, a newcomer from London, records the story in his diary after hearing it from his housekeeper Nelly Dean. Because many of Nelly's characters are living people whom Lockwood meets during the course of his stay, and because daily life interrupts her tale several times—a hiatus of nine months postpones the narration of the final events—Brontë also creates a troubling, distorted sense of time. The present world is haunted not only by past events; the novel is also framed by a pair of unresolved ghostly visitations which leave the two most incredulous characters—Lockwood and Nelly Dean—wondering at the spiritual mysteries of Wuthering Heights.

The novel begins with Lockwood's diary entry from the winter of 1801. As a new tenant of the Thrushcross Grange estate, he pays a visit to his landlord, Heathcliff. Both the neighboring estate, Wuthering Heights—a grim thick-walled farmhouse—and his host are singularly unwelcoming. Within minutes of his arrival, an angry pack of dogs attacks him. Heathcliff and the servant Joseph belatedly and ungraciously save him and Lockwood leaves, disgusted. On a second visit he meets Heathcliff's beautiful but unfriendly widowed daughter-in-law, Catherine, and her sullen, illiterate cousin Hareton Earnshaw. Lockwood offends his hosts by mistaking Catherine for Heathcliff's wife and then for Hareton's wife, and he poses a further inconvenience by finding he must stay overnight: a snowstorm begun during his visit prevents his departure.

His hosts make no effort to accommodate him until the housekeeper, at the beginning of **chapter three**, shows him to a small bedchamber. Lockwood finds the name of Catherine carved on the old-fashioned paneled bed and discovers some old schoolbooks, including a fragment of what proves to be the late Cathy Earnshaw's diary. Her youthful scribblings describe a painful Sunday under the guardianship of her older brother, Hindley. The interminable preaching of Joseph (a servant whom Lockwood himself has met), memorization of Bible passages, Hindley's anger, and her imprisonment in the washroom make up the familiar pattern of her day. In the end she breaks off, deciding to escape to the moors with her playmate Heathcliff.

Lockwood nods off and is plagued by nightmares. He dreams that he hears a tree knocking on the window and that he breaks the glass to tear off the branch. Reaching out into the storm he is grabbed by an ice-cold hand. He sees a child's face outside, and a voice identifying itself as Catherine Linton begs to be let in. When he panics and tries to release the grip by rubbing the spirit's wrist against the broken glass, his terror at the sight of the blood jolts him awake with a loud yell. The noise rouses Heathcliff. Horrified to find Lockwood in his dead beloved's bedchamber, he orders him to leave. Lockwood then unwillingly witnesses Heathcliff's desperate anguish. Thinking himself alone, his host throws open the windows and tearfully begs Cathy's ghost to enter.

Heathcliff reappears for breakfast transformed from wretched lover to an angry, brutish master, roughly upbraiding Catherine, who lashes back. Lockwood leaves the grim household with renewed disgust. He catches a bad cold on his journey home. For most of the remaining novel (**chapters four through thirty**) he lies in bed listening eagerly to his housekeeper's story of how Wuthering Heights arrived at its present state.

Nelly was a servant at Wuthering Heights when she was little, growing up with the Earnshaw family's children. She begins her story with the arrival of Heathcliff, when Hindley Earnshaw was fourteen and his sister, Cathy, was six. Their father returned from a trip to London with a mysterious, ragged gypsy child, whom the family first greeted with horror.

Grudgingly accepted, Heathcliff, as he was called, became the master's favorite and grew to be Cathy's ally and Hindley's hated enemy. Cathy was a willful, spontaneous child, "[h]er spirits . . . always at high-water mark," constantly in trouble or playing the "little mistress." Heathcliff was stoically hardened and single-minded, in one instance withstanding Hindley's brutal thrashing to blackmail him into giving up his pony.

Cathy's mother dies, Hindley leaves for college, and the increasingly authoritarian master dies three years later. At his father's funeral Hindley arrives married to a weak, silly woman. He takes over Wuthering Heights and immediately cuts off Heathcliff's education, forcing him to work as a destitute farm laborer. Cathy also suffers under her cruel brother, but their punishments only make the two friends more reckless and more devoted to each other.

One Sunday evening (here in **chapter six** Nelly's story adroitly picks up where Cathy's diary had left off) Cathy and Heathcliff escape to the moors and sneak up to the neighboring Linton estate, Thrushcross Grange. They see the spoiled children Edgar and Isabella through the window in the throes of a tantrum. Before they can leave the guard dogs attack; one grabs Cathy's ankle and the two are caught. When they are brought inside, Edgar recognizes Cathy and the family rushes to her aid. Meanwhile dark, ragged Heathcliff is declared "unfit for a decent house" and thrown out, leaving Cathy surrounded by a doting family.

This episode contrasts two distinctive spaces in Brontë's novel. Reversing anticipated associations, she describes the cruel, unsheltering moor as a savage earthly paradise where Cathy and Heathcliff are free and equal. But the Lintons' comfortable parlor, "a splendid place carpeted with crimson, and crimson covered chairs and tables," is a site of unhappiness, a wrongheaded, restrictive heaven. When Cathy abandons the moor, her shared world with Heathcliff, the act has biblical connotations, showing her choice as a fall from innocence.

In **chapter seven** Cathy returns at Christmas; after five weeks at Thrushcross Grange, she has become a dignified young lady dressed in furs and silks. Heathcliff, made acutely aware of their different social stations, confides to Nelly that he envies Edgar's looks and breeding. Cathy is torn between her new and old friends, attempting at a Christmas dinner to play a gay hostess to the Lintons but inwardly suffering when Heathcliff, in anger, throws sauce on Edgar and is banished from the table.

Nelly relates how Heathcliff's cruel mistreatment escalates when Hindley's wife dies after giving birth to a son. The husband's grief drives him to drink and gambling. Nelly cares for the boy, Hareton, and watches the dissipation of the once prominent family. "I could not half tell what an infernal house we had," she remembers. Unchecked, Cathy leads a double life, reckless at home but charming to the Lintons. Her mask drops one afternoon when Edgar comes courting (**chapter eight**) and Cathy, incited by a jealous Heathcliff and unindulgent Nelly, takes out her rage on Hareton. Edgar intervenes and she boxes his ear. Shocked, he tries to leave and Cathy breaks into tears. Despite Nelly's prompting, he cannot tear himself away. Their fight leads to an open declaration of love.

The day of crisis continues violently. Hindley comes home drunk, threatens Nelly with a carving knife, and nearly drops Hareton to his death. He showers Heathcliff with more abuse, and Heathcliff vows revenge. That evening an angry but half-repentant Cathy seeks Nelly's advice. She has accepted Edgar's proposal of marriage but feels uneasy. In an important speech in **chapter nine** she explains why the engagement makes her so unhappy. She tells how she had once dreamed she was in heaven, and she had been so miserable and homesick that the angry angels had flung her back to earth, where she awoke on the heath "sobbing for joy." She insists that marrying Edgar would be like going to that heaven; she would be unhappy and grieve for Heathcliff, her second half. She proclaims, "He's more myself than I am! Whatever our souls are made of, his and mine are the same; and Linton's is as different as a moonbeam from lightning, or frost from fire." The speech recalls the imagery of the sixth chapter, reinforcing the portrayal of the Linton's house as an unhappy, restrictive heaven. It also presents love, unconventionally for its time, as a passionate union of equals and soul mates.

As Nelly listens, she notices that Heathcliff has overheard from an adjoining room but has left before Cathy's admission of love, stung by her assertion that to marry him penniless would degrade her. His departure is discovered at the evening meal. A summer thunderstorm breaks out. Nature, as is often the case in Brontë's world, acts here as an empathetic participant in the crisis of characters who are themselves so closely associated with their surrounding landscape. Cathy, distraught, spends the night looking for Heathcliff. In the morning, drenched and grief-ridden, she becomes delirious and falls gravely ill. He does not return, and a long period of convalescence ensues. Nelly passes quickly over the events of the next three years: Cathy's recovery, the death of both Linton parents, Hindley's continued life of debauchery, and Cathy's marriage. Nelly goes to live with her mistress at Thrushcross Grange, regretfully leaving Hareton in the hands of his negligent father.

Here (**chapter ten**) Nelly interrupts her story, leaving Lockwood in a weak, fretful state. Several characters from her narrative come to pay visits, oddly telescoping the passage of time. They include the doctor who had overseen Hareton's birth and Cathy's delirium and Heathcliff himself. After four irksome weeks Lockwood calls Nelly to finish her story.

Resuming, Nelly skims over the first happy year of Cathy's marriage, when an indulgent Edgar and Isabella humored her every wish. "It was not the thorn bending to the honeysuckles, but the honeysuckles embracing the thorn." Heathcliff soon shatters this peace. He returns one September evening, approaching Nelly, who at first does not recognize the tall, well-dressed gentleman in the garden. Cathy is overwhelmed with joy, but the enraptured reunion of his wife and guest strains Edgar's politeness to its limit. He unwillingly tolerates Heathcliff's continued visits. Much to Nelly's surprise Heathcliff moves in with his old enemy Hindley, who has lost to him at cards and is eager to reclaim his debts. Meanwhile, eighteen-year-old Isabella develops a crush on Heathcliff, eventually divulging her secret to Cathy. Cathy contemptuously warns her sister-in-law of the dangers of her friend. Heathcliff, she says, is "an unreclaimed creature, without refinement, without cultivation; an arid wilderness of furze and whinstone. I'd as soon put that little canary into the park on a winter's day, as recommend you to bestow your heart on him!" Isabella insists that Cathy is simply jealous, and stung by this rebuke, Cathy cruelly reveals her sister-in-law's secret to Heathcliff. He admits he detests her "maukish waxen face," so like Edgar's, but learns that she would be her brother's heir were Edgar to die without a son.

In **chapter eleven**, Nelly is troubled by premonitions of a crisis and visits the Heights. Hareton has turned into an angry, violent child taught by Heathcliff to curse his own father. On returning to Thrushcross Grange, Nelly catches Heathcliff embracing Isabella in the garden. Cathy is called and an argument ensues. Heathcliff accuses Cathy of having treated him "infernally" but claims he seeks no revenge on her, his tyrant, only on those weaker than himself.

When Nelly promptly tells Edgar of what has transpired, he tries to throw Heathcliff out of the house. His guest is incredulous: "Cathy, this lamb of yours threatens like a bull. . . . It is in danger of splitting its skull against my knuckles." The confrontation breaks up when Linton leaves for reinforcements and Heathcliff escapes through the back. Cathy, angry at both men, confides to Nelly that she intends to hurt them through her own self-destruction: "I'll try to break their hearts by breaking my own." When Edgar returns, Cathy explodes with hysterical rage. Nelly is first convinced that she is acting, but when Cathy overhears this speculation, she starts up with renewed fury and locks herself in her room. In the novel, her diabolical temper, which sends her husband cowering, is matched only by Heathcliff's pitch of vengeful anger.

Cathy's self-imprisonment and starvation last for three days. When she finally lets Nelly enter (**chapter twelve**), she is weak and half-delirious, though still angry with Edgar. As she slips in and out of lucidity, she tells Nelly of her anguish, continually thinking she is back at the Heights and then realizing her prison-like married state. "Oh, I'm burning!" she cries. "I wish I were out of doors! I wish I were a girl again, half savage and hardy, and free . . . and laughing at injuries, not maddening under them!" Her premonition of losing the invulnerable paradise of her youth has proved all too true. As she opens the windows and calls for Heathcliff, Edgar enters. He is astonished to see her so deteriorated and angrily sends Nelly for the doctor. In the town she hears a rumor that Heathcliff has eloped with Isabella. The news is confirmed the next morning, and Edgar, crushed by his wife's state, quietly disowns his sister without an attempt at pursuit.

The emotional storm of the evening is followed, as after Heathcliff's first departure, by a recuperative lull in the story. Two months of Edgar's attentive care find Cathy well enough to sit but permanently weakened. The reader learns that they are expecting a child. Meanwhile, Heathcliff and Isabella return to the Heights. Edgar refuses Isabella's note, so she writes a long letter to Nelly, which is read to Lockwood in **chapter thirteen**. Isabella tells of her husband's appalling cruelty, the primitive conditions of the cold, stony Heights, and its hostile occupants, Hindley, Hareton, and Joseph. She asks Nelly, "Is Mr. Heathcliff a man? If so, is he mad? If not, is he a devil?" Nelly visits, finding Isabella utterly destitute and turned as cruel and vicious as her husband. Before Nelly leaves, Heathcliff forces her to promise to help him see Cathy.

Heathcliff's speech to Nelly relies on a repeated motif from the novel, using imagery from nature to describe a character. Cathy had likened Heathcliff's soul to the arid wilderness of the moors, while Nelly described the Lintons as honeysuckles, cultivated and fragile. Here Heathcliff proclaims of Edgar's meager love: "He might as well plant an oak in a flower-pot and expect it to thrive, as imagine he can restore her to vigor in the soil of his shallow cares!" These metaphors reinforce the contrast of wilderness and cultivation that dominates the novel.

While Edgar nurses Cathy at the Grange, Heathcliff roams the gardens outside. In **chapter fifteen**, Heathcliff spies his chance when Edgar leaves for Sunday church. Cathy is a beautiful, haunting vision of her former self. Heathcliff enters, grasping her in his arms. In the scene that follows, both lovers vindictively accuse and forgive each other, realizing that Cathy is going to die. She says she hopes Heathcliff will suffer as he has made her suffer and declares herself eager to escape life, her "shattered prison." In a second impassioned embrace Heathcliff asks Cathy why she had despised him and betrayed her heart. Meanwhile, Edgar returns from church and as Cathy, mad with grief, clings to her lover, Nelly tries to force Heathcliff to leave. They are discovered, Cathy falls in a faint, and Edgar forgets everything to attend to her. That evening Cathy gives birth to a daughter and dies without regaining full consciousness.

While the house is in mourning, Nelly finds Heathcliff in the garden. He is angry and unrepentant. His one prayer is that Cathy will not rest in peace while he is living. "You said I killed you—haunt me then!" he calls to her. Cathy is buried unconventionally in a corner of the churchyard overlooking the heath.

The grief-stricken house is interrupted in **chapter seventeen** by the giddy entrance of Isabella, who has run coatless through a spring snowstorm from the Heights. She sees only Nelly before continuing her escape, telling her of the violent past days at the Heights. Hindley had tried to murder Heathcliff, who had cut his attacker badly and then beaten him. The next morning Isabella had taunted Heathcliff, accusing him of having killed Cathy. In anger he had thrown a knife at her, cutting the side of her head, and she had fled, wildly happy to be free. Isabella leaves and Nelly eventually hears news that she has settled near London and given birth to a sickly child named Linton. Six months later Hindley dies, drunk to the last and so deeply in debt to Heathcliff that his son, Hareton, is forced into dependency on his father's worst enemy.

Hindley's death brings the events of the first half of the novel to a close. While this part has a Gothic pitch sustained by its two passionate protagonists, the second half begins in the tone of a fairy tale. In a strange reversal, Heathcliff becomes the vengeful, scheming villain, while a new romantic triangle, uncannily reminiscent of his own, unfolds among the second generation. **Chapter eighteen** begins with an idyllic interlude, during which Catherine Linton, Cathy's daughter, grows to adolescence. Nelly is her nursemaid and a saddened

Edgar becomes a loving, watchful father. Catherine has both her mother's willful high spirits and her father's tenderness. She lives a secluded life for thirteen years, ignorant of Wuthering Heights or its inhabitants. Then Edgar is called to Isabella's deathbed, leaving Catherine for three weeks. Against Nelly's orders she rides out past the park walls and comes across Wuthering Heights. Nelly finds her happily drinking tea with the housekeeper and a tall, bashful eighteen-year-old Hareton. Catherine ignores Nelly's scolding but leaves after offending a smitten Hareton by mistaking him for the master and then treating him like a servant. Nelly swears Catherine to secrecy, worried of Edgar's anger.

Isabella dies and Edgar returns with her peevish child. Catherine dotes on her cousin Linton, but when Heathcliff demands his son, Edgar has no choice but to comply. The next morning Nelly sneaks Linton to the Heights before Catherine can learn of his fate. The boy is terrified of his father, but Heathcliff, although dearly disgusted with his progeny, tells Nelly he plans to pamper Linton, the heir to Edgar's estate. Reports from the housekeeper confirm Nelly's suspicion that Linton is a selfish, spoiled inmate.

In **chapter twenty-one**, Catherine, on her sixteenth birthday, goes for a walk with Nelly and meets Heathcliff and Hareton on the heath. Heathcliff, against Nelly's warnings, cajoles Catherine into visiting Wuthering Heights. Catherine is overjoyed to find her long-lost cousin. Linton, for his part, has grown into a languid self-absorbed teenager, still in delicate health. Heathcliff confides to Nelly that he hopes the two will marry, as he worries that Linton may not live to inherit Edgar's estate. Hareton suffers under Catherine's snubs and leaves angrily when Linton makes fun of his illiteracy. Heathcliff brags that he has reduced Hindley's son to the same destitution as Hindley had once reduced him.

When Edgar learns of Catherine's visit, he forbids further trips to the Heights, so Catherine begins a clandestine correspondence with her cousin. Nelly soon discovers her secret stash of love letters and forces her to burn them. Several months later, Catherine, walking with Nelly by the park wall, slips over to retrieve a fallen hat and is accosted by Heathcliff. He accuses her of breaking Linton's heart, insisting his son is dying. Catherine determines to pay a secret visit. Catherine and Nelly's visit takes place in **chapter twenty-three**. Sickly and self-absorbed, Linton tortures Catherine by exaggerating a violent coughing fit and forces her to stay and pamper him. Riding home, Nelly catches a bad cold. She later discovers that during her three weeks in bed Catherine had visited the Heights almost every evening. She extracts a confession from Catherine after catching her returning from another visit. Catherine tells of Linton's temper and Hareton's bashful attentions and jealousy. Heathcliff appears to have been a hidden but watchful audience.

Nelly reports Catherine's visits to her father, who again puts an end to them. The months pass and Catherine turns seventeen. Her father, his health failing, worries for her future and agrees to let the cousins meet on the moors. At the first meeting, Linton is so weak he can barely walk; he dozes off but wakes terrified that Nelly and Catherine should leave before the allotted time.

Catherine is saddened by the meeting, and the next week, in **chapter twenty-seven**, her father is so much worse that she sets out for her visit unwillingly. She meets Linton who is almost crazed with fear. Heathcliff appears, Linton falls limp, and Catherine is forced to help escort him to his house, while Nelly follows, scolding. At the Heights, Heathcliff, in his strongest incarnation of a Gothic villain, kidnaps Catherine. He locks the door and slaps her for resisting. Linton selfishly refuses to help her. Heathcliff forces Nelly and Catherine to stay overnight and in the morning takes Catherine away. Nelly remains locked up for five days. When she is set free, she learns that Heathcliff has forced Catherine to marry Linton. Nelly leaves to get help and finds Edgar on his deathbed. That evening Catherine escapes and is able to sit by her father as he dies.

After the funeral, Heathcliff arrives to take Catherine back to the Heights to nurse Linton, forbidding Nelly to see her. He also tells a horrified Nelly that, after Edgar's burial, he had dug up and opened Cathy's coffin. He tells how he has been haunted by her presence since the night of her funeral, when he had gone to the graveyard to dig up her coffin and had heard a distinct sigh at his ear. From that moment he had felt her presence constantly. "And when I slept in her chamber . . ." he recalls, "I couldn't lie there; for the moment I closed my eyes, she was either outside the window, or sliding back the panels, or entering the room. . . ." The sight of her still unmarred beauty has eased his tortured nerves.

Nelly learns only through hearsay of her mistress's new life. Catherine is forced to nurse Linton alone and lives a sleepless, grim existence until he dies. The experience turns her bitter and hostile. She rarely leaves her room unless driven out by cold. In the kitchen she antagonizes the housekeeper and reviles Hareton's acts of kindness. This dreary state of affairs brings the story up to the present: Lockwood has witnessed such scenes himself during his visits.

Here (**chapter thirty-one**) the frame narrative intervenes again. Lockwood's journal now dates from the second week of January 1802; he has recovered from his cold and is determined to leave his isolation for London. He pays a last visit to the Heights, meeting a low-spirited Catherine, who mourns for her old life and her books and cruelly taunts Hareton for his attempts to read. Heathcliff's entrance cuts an admiring Lockwood's overtures to Catherine short, and he soon leaves. The diary then leaps eight months to September of that year. Visiting in the neighborhood, Lockwood finds himself near Thrushcross Grange and decides to spend the night. He finds Nelly has moved to the Heights, and on going to see her, he learns that Heathcliff is dead and Catherine is engaged to marry Hareton. He first comes upon the lovers engrossed in a reading lesson. Hareton, happy and well groomed, dotes on his beautiful, playful teacher. Regretting his own lost chance, Lockwood sneaks off to find Nelly and hear the end of the story.

Nelly had been summoned to the Heights soon after Lockwood's departure. Her mistress, first delighted to see her, had soon grown irritable and impatient. She constantly sought out Hareton's company in order to tease him. She had tried underhandedly to entice him to read, but he had stubbornly ignored her. Finally she had apologized to him, sealing her peace offering with a kiss and a book, gifts he could barely accept in his bashful confusion.

At the time this new alliance is formed, Heathcliff has begun to act strange and distant, increasingly attracted by a mysterious, otherworldly force. He forgets to eat or sleep. One morning, after spending the night wandering the heath, he tells Nelly, "Last night I was on the threshold of hell. Today I am within sight of my heaven" (**chapter thirty-three**).

That morning he is startled by the sight of the happy couple, Catherine and Hareton, who both share a marked likeness to the late Cathy—Hareton in particular resembles his aunt. Heathcliff confides to Nelly that Hareton reminds him uncannily of his former self. Here he makes explicit an important theme of the novel: the repeated pattern of the love affairs. Heathcliff admits to Nelly that the attachment is a "poor conclusion" to his plans, but his altered state has sapped his desire for revenge. "I don't care for striking, I can't take the trouble to raise my hand," he says.

Heathcliff's torturous, distracted existence continues. That evening Nelly takes fright on finding him transfixed in a deep reverie with ghastly, sunken eyes and a menacing smile. His nocturnal wanderings continue, and during the day he locks himself in Cathy's paneled bedroom. After a further night of wild storms, Nelly breaks into the room to find the windows open, and when she pulls back the panels, she is met with a fierce, unblinking gaze—Heathcliff is dead. To the scandal of the community, Heathcliff is buried next to Catherine. The country folk doubt that he rests in peace, claiming that they have seen his ghost walking the moors. Nelly is skeptical, although she has recently met a young shepherd boy on the heath who, sobbing, reported that he had just seen Heathcliff walking with a woman. The book ends with this final suggestion that Cathy and Heathcliff have been reunited in their moorland paradise.

In her novel, Brontë thus allows the love affair of the second generation to be played out as a muted and happy version of the first. Nonetheless, it is Cathy and Heathcliff's love story that remains branded on the reader's memory. Their fiery example idealizes love as an attraction of equal, explosive forces, as a passion too savagely strong for the confines of cultivated society, and ultimately as a bond more powerful than life itself.

Critical Views

MELVIN R. WATSON ON HEATHCLIFF'S COMPLEX PERSONALITY

Wuthering Heights, then, is a psychological study of an elemental man whose soul is torn between love and hate. He is a creature about whose past nothing is known. A dark, dirty beggar, he was picked up on the Liverpool streets by Mr. Earnshaw and brought to the secluded part of the world known as the moors, where he has ample space to work out his destiny. Only the elemental passions of love and hate receive any development in the elemental environment by which he was molded. His strength of will and steadfastness of purpose he brought with him to the moors, but there they were prevented by external events from following their natural course. There he was hardened by his physical surroundings, toughened and embittered by the harsh treatment of Hindley, disillusioned by what he considered the treachery of Catherine, on whom he had poured love out of his boundless store. Then he resolves to even scores by crushing everyone who has stood in his way, everyone who has helped to thwart his happiness, the specter of which haunts him for seventeen long years during which he works out the venom which has accumulated in his soul. As soon as part of the venom is removed and the day of happiness begins to dawn, he no longer has the will to keep up his torturing.

This is a daring theme, subject to much misinterpretation, for during most of the action Heathcliff performs like a villain or like a hero who has consciously chosen evil for his companion. When completely understood, however, he is neither an Iago for whom evil is a divinity nor a Macbeth who consciously chooses evil because of his overpowering ambition, but rather a Hamlet without Hamlet's fatal irresolution. Like Hamlet, he was precipitated into a world in which he saw cruelty and unfaithfulness operating. His dilemma was not Hamlet's, for he has no father to avenge or mother to protect, but in a way

34

he has evil thrust upon him if he is to survive among harsh surroundings. And Heathcliff was not one to hesitate when faced with an alternative, however tragic the consequences might be.

Though Heathcliff is not perhaps more sinned against than sinning, his actions are produced by the distortion of his natural personality. This distortion had already begun when Mr. Earnshaw brought him into Wuthering Heights, a "dirty, ragged, black-haired child." Already he was inured to hardship and blows; already he uncomplainingly accepted suffering, as when he had the measles, and ill treatment from Hindley if he got what he wanted. From the very first he showed great courage, steadfastness, and love. But with Mr. Earnshaw's death Hindley has the power to degrade Heathcliff to the status of a servant. A weak, vindictive character, as cruel as Heathcliff without Heathcliff's strength, Hindley prepares for his own destruction by his inhumanity to Heathcliff and the other inhabitants of the Heights. Though Heathcliff was forced down to an animal level, he took a silent delight in watching his persecutor sinking also into a life of debauchery. Nor was he alone, for he had Cathy, on whom he poured his devotion and love. They were inseparable. On the moors by day or in the chimney corner by night, they chatted and dreamed whenever Heathcliff was not busy with the chores. But the visit to Thrushcross Grange introduced Cathy to another world to which she opened her arms, and that world contained Edgar Linton. Edgar held a superficial attraction for Cathy which Heathcliff could never understand and which he feared, for, having possessed Cathy for some years, he feared losing even part of her attention. The final blow, a blow which turns Heathcliff from sullen acquiescence to tragic determination, comes when Cathy confesses to Ellen [Nelly] her infatuation with Edgar and her resolve to marry him so that she and Heathcliff can escape from the repressive world of Wuthering Heights. Not once did she think of giving up Heathcliff, but Heathcliff inadvertently overhears only the first part of the conversation. Cathy has deserted him for a mess of pottage, for fine clothes and refined manners; she is ashamed of his rough exterior, of his lack of polish; she would be degraded to marry him as he is. Heathcliff doesn't stay to hear Cathy confess her oneness with him:

If all else perished, and *he* remained, I should still continue to be; and if all else remained, and he were annihilated, the universe would turn to a mighty stranger: I should not seem a part of it. My love for Linton is like the foliage in the woods: time will change it, I'm well aware, as winter changes the trees. My love for Heathcliff resembles the eternal rocks beneath: a source of little visible delight, but necessary. Nelly, I am Heathcliff. He's always, always in my mind: not as a pleasure, any more than I am always a pleasure to myself, but as my own being.

His mind is made up. If love alone is insufficient to hold Cathy, he will secure the necessary money and polish; if his only happiness is to be snatched from him, he will turn to hate; and now not only Hindley will be the object of his wrath, but Edgar also. As long as he had Cathy, his worldly condition, his suffering, was as nothing; without her, all is chaff to be trampled underfoot.

For three years, during which he vanishes from sight, he prepares himself, the poison in his system increasing all the time until love is submerged in a sea of hate which he must drain off before love can reassert itself. Union with Cathy is his one desire. Since physical union is made impossible by her death—not that it was ever important,—the union must be spiritual, but the world and the people of the world must be subjugated before such happiness can be achieved. The course is set, the wind is strong, the bark is sturdy, the journey long. For seventeen years Heathcliff wreaks his vengeance on Hindley, Edgar, and Isabella and on their children Hareton, young Cathy, and Linton. The account of the trip is not pretty. Even in the love scenes before the elder Cathy's death there is a savage passion which strikes terror to the heart of the beholder, unlike any other scenes in the course of English fiction; and before the masochistic treatment of Isabella, Hareton, young Cathy, and Linton we cringe. Here is a man haunted by a ghost of happiness for which he must exorcise his soul, a soul filled with accumulated hatred. That he ceases his reign of terror before Hareton and young Cathy have been completely broken is due not to any loss of spiritual strength but to the realization that the end of the voyage is near, that the tempest is subsiding, and that reunion with Cathy is about to be consummated. In Heathcliff one looks in vain for Christian morals or virtues; his is a primitive, pagan soul; yet love conquers even a Heathcliff in the end—after his soul has been purged of the hate in and with which he has lived for decades. The evil that he does springs not from a love of evil itself, but from the thwarting of the natural processes of love.

Muriel Spark and Derek Stanford on Characterization in the Novel

In a similar way, Catherine's delirium marks a turning-point in her existence. Not only does it indicate the crisis of her illness—after which the currents of her life shift their direction and flow towards death—but it marks also a mental change. It serves as the symbol of a trauma, the experiencing of which has led her nature wholly to reject her husband's love. Until that moment, her affection for Edgar had been real though limited in scope. Physically, she had found him attractive; and if there had never been any question of her sharing with him that sympathy of soul which she had enjoyed with Heathcliff, Edgar's tenderness and kindness had given him no small claim upon her heart.

> "What you touch at present you may"; she tells her husband, who comes to see her during her illness, after a quarrel, "but my soul will be on that hill-top before you lay hands on me again. I don't want you, Edgar: I'm past wanting you."

What has happened is that her love for Heathcliff—buried for so long—has burst to the surface again, on his reappearance. But in the trauma which is expressed by her delirium, we find few references to the grown Heathcliff. It is to the Heathcliff of her youth that her wandering mind returns. Plucking the feathers from her pillow, she ruminates fancifully upon them:

"And here is a moor-cock's; and this—I should know it among a thousand—it's a lapwing's. Bonny bird; wheeling over our heads in the middle of the moor. It wanted to get to its nest, for the clouds had touched the swells, and it felt rain coming. This feather was picked up from the heath, the bird was not shot: we saw its nest in the winter, full of little skeletons. Heathcliff set a trap over it, and the old ones dare not come. I made him promise he'd never shoot a lapwing after that, and he didn't. Yes, here are more! Did he shoot my lapwings, Nelly? Are they red, any of them! Let me look."

But the course of her spirit is setting towards death, as much as to the object of her rekindled love; and Heathcliff the boy, and Heathcliff the man exist together in her mind when she looks from her bedroom at Thrushcross Grange, imagining that she can see the candle in her window at *Wuthering Heights* (some: five miles away, and quite invisible):

"Look!" she cried eagerly, "that's my room with the candle in it, and the trees swaying before it: and the other candle is in Joseph's garret. Joseph sits up late, doesn't he? He's waiting till I come home that he may lock the gate. Well, he'll wait a little while yet. It's a rough journey, and a sad heart to travel it; and we must pass by Gimmerton Kirk, to go that journey! We've braved its ghosts often together, and dared each other to stand among the graves and ask them to come. But, Heathcliff, if I dare you now, will you venture? If you do, I'll keep you. I'll not lie there by myself: they may bury me twelve feet deep, and throw the church down over me, but I won't rest till you are with me. I never will!"

The full stream of her mind has turned back towards the past. The present—save as a dimension of pain—possesses no reality for her. The future holds only a sense of death. . . .

In contrast to this dramatic portrayal of character, we have in the minor figures of *Wuthering Heights* a static presentation of personality. Joseph, the serving-man, and Nelly Dean, the house-keeper, do not change their words or ways one iota. They grow older, and in Nelly Dean's case the occasional play of nostalgia over memories of her youth is sometimes evoked. But she is "a canty dame"; a busy, kindly, practical body, seldom giving to thinking of herself. In her narrative of the chief characters, we have a mirror held up to the past, a mirror whose glass is sometimes dimmed with sadness for those whom it reflects, but hardly on its own behalf at all.

Joseph, the serving-man, is presented yet more simply. Apart from his attachment to Wuthering Heights, it is hard to imagine him possessed of a past. He is, pre-eminently, portrayed 'in the flat'. Both he and Nelly Dean are bound by ties of association to the environment of the drama, and this rootedness in the place gives them an added stability in the way that their image affects the imagination. "My mother had nursed Mr. Hindley Earnshaw that was Hareton's father", Nelly Dean tells Mr. Lockwood. While speaking of her early days she says, "I ran errands, and helped to make hay, and hung about the farm ready for anything that anybody would set me to." Our sense of the permanence of these characters may have owed something to Emily's reading of Wordsworth, in whom the idea of the stabilising influence of one given place in the growth of character is often enough encountered.

But the sense of permanence which Nelly Dean and Joseph evoke is out of all proportion to the miscellany of moods and mannerisms which go to make up a character in life. They are largely functional figures (Nelly's activity being that of narrator, whilst Joseph's purpose appears to be that of creating a kind of humorous relief). This relief, it is true, is of a singularly unbuoyant order. It is a grim and narrow humour that we get from this Calvinistic servitor. "The wearisomest self-righteous Pharisee that ever ransacked a Bible to rate the promises to himself and fling the curses to his neighbours" is Nelly Dean's description of him. But for all the unpleasantness of his nature, and the canting sententiousness of his speech, we must admit that the language he uses shows Emily a master of dialect. Compared with Joseph's native invective, Heathcliff's talk is rhetorically Byronic. Joseph—the most undeveloped character in this novel—expresses himself more authentically than any of the other more complex figures. No doubt there is a touch of caricature in Joseph, through whose creation Emily was able to publish her scorn of Calvinism, and so get even with her aunt, who was always thrusting such doctrines down her throat. But, I think, there is more than satire in Joseph. Emily, though intellectually rebellious, was attracted by harshness and narrowness;[4] and when this went combined with the local vigour of an altogether unsophisticated speech, I suspect she found the material fascinating. In Joseph's remarks and monologues, she certainly achieved one of the most racy uses of rustic speech in English fiction.

Of the major characters in this book, I have no doubt that Catherine is the greatest—the fullest and most original in creation. Besides her uniqueness, Heathcliff appears as a tedious stock Byronic figure—his mouth filled with oaths and his fist raised to strike—a perversely idealised adolescent in a tantrum. How many lines of misanthropic rant by the author of *The Corsair*, *The Giaour*, and *Lara* might be applied to Heathcliff's condition!

For I have buried one and all,
Who loved me in a human shape;
And the whole earth would henceforth be
A wider prison unto me.

"I learned to love despair," says one of Byron's heroes; and despair and revenge make up the gamut of Heathcliff's emotions after Catherine's death. To recognise the 'note' of the Byronic type in Byron is to have recognised all one needs to know of the character of Heathcliff, who is Byron in prose dress.

Catherine, it is true, has a prototype in literature; though it is unlikely that Emily used the original figure as a base for her creation. Or if she did, she so developed the traits of character and their outcome in action, that there can be no suggestion of a copy. None the less, it is interesting to notice that Emily's heroine bears the same name as Shakespeare's Katharina, in

The Taming of the Shrew. But Emily's shrew is a tragic one; and Cathy (her daughter, who—in some ways—completes her mother's emotional intention) is not overcome by ring-master tactics but by Hareton's independent nature, thawing out into co-operation and affection.

But if Catherine appears as the unbroken filly, the shrew who is not tamed by her husband Edgar (even though we are given to understand she loves him), this is only one aspect of her make-up and a merely symptomatic one at that. For Catherine, in fact, is a curious case of self-love carried to the extreme; the degree of her obsession giving an almost paranoic quality to what she observes. When she lies with a self-induced frenzy, weak from want of food, she seems at times to be near to arriving at the truth about herself:

> ". . . I begin to fancy you don't like me", she tells Nelly Dean during her illness. "How strange! I thought, though everybody hated and despised each other, they could not avoid loving me. And they have all turned to enemies in a few hours. *They* have, I'm positive—the people *here*."

The falsehood or illusion lies, of course, in imagining that nobody could avoid loving her. They had not suddenly changed to enemies merely because for a moment she was able to see that they were not infatuated. She had chosen to believe that everybody was under her spell, and when she sees that spell denied, she concludes that her faithful *devotées* have now become her adversaries. Her whole perspective is egoistic and unreal.

This ambiguous double-vision in which Catherine sees yet does not see herself—in which she recognises the truth and then straightaway distorts it—has its symbolic counter-part in the scene where she catches sight of her face in the mirror but does not identify it as her own. To her, it appears a strange and frightening countenance—*because she has willed not to recognise herself*. Catherine, indeed, represents the spirit of chaos in human affairs. Only in nature does she find that freedom which her will demands; only on the moors does she discover that liberty from personal responsibility which her unbridled egoism insists upon.

And as she accepts no principle of inter-dependence during her life, so in death she wishes to avoid it. She wants to be buried "in the open air, with a headstone", and not in the Lintons' chapel where her husband's family have been laid.

Note

4. That Emily well understood the nature of such a repulsive sympathy can be shown from many passages in her works. "But no brutality disgusted her: I suspect she has an innate admiration of" says Heathcliff of his wife Isabella.

J. HILLIS MILLER ON THE SIGNIFICANCE OF ANIMAL IMAGERY

The opening chapters of *Wuthering Heights* introduce the reader, through the intermediary of the narrator, to a set of people living in the state of nature as it is defined in "The Butterfly." This state also matches that of the Gondal poems, with their wars and rebellions and sadistic cruelties. In Gondal, as in the country of *Wuthering Heights*, every man's hand is against his neighbor.

Lockwood's discovery of the nature of life at Wuthering Heights coincides with his step-by-step progress into the house itself. On his two visits he crosses various thresholds: the outer gate, the door of the house, the door into the kitchen, the stairs and halls leading to an upstairs room. Finally he enters the interior of the interior, the oaken closet with a bed in it which stands in a corner of this inner room. Wuthering Heights is presented as a kind of Chinese box of enclosures within enclosures. The house is like the novel itself, with its intricate structure of flashbacks, time shifts, multiple perspectives, and narrators within narrators. However far we penetrate toward the center of Wuthering Heights there are still further recesses within. When Lockwood finally gets inside the family sitting-room he can hear "a chatter of tongues, and a clatter of culinary utensils, deep within,"[14] and Joseph can be heard mumbling indistinctly in the "depths of the cellar" (5). This domestic interior is, by subtle linguistic touches, identified with the interior of a human body, and therefore with another human spirit. Lockwood's progress toward the interior of Wuthering Heights matches his unwitting progress toward the spiritual secrets it hides. Just as the "narrow windows" of Wuthering Heights are "deeply set in the wall" (2), so Heathcliff's "black eyes withdraw . . . suspiciously under their brows" (1), and Lockwood's entrance into the house is his inspection of its "anatomy" (3).

The nature of human life within this "penetralium" (3) is precisely defined by the animals Lockwood finds there. The shadowy recesses of these strange rooms are alive with ferocious dogs: "In an arch, under the dresser, reposed a huge, liver-coloured bitch pointer surrounded by a swarm of squealing puppies; and other dogs, haunted other recesses" (3). Lockwood tries to pet this liver-colored bitch, but her lip is "curled up, and her white teeth watering for a snatch" (5), and later when, left alone, he makes faces at the dogs, they leap from their various hiding places and attack him in a pack. In a moment the hearth is "an absolute tempest of worrying and yelping" (6). The storm which blows at the exterior of the house and gives it its name (2) is echoed by the storm within the house, a tempest whose ultimate source, it may be, is the people living there. Lockwood's encounter with Heathcliff's dogs is really his first encounter with the true nature of their owner, as Heathcliff himself suggests when he says: "Guests are so exceedingly rare in this house that I and my dogs, I am willing to own, hardly know how to receive them" (6).

The animal imagery used throughout *Wuthering Heights* is one of the chief ways in which the spiritual strength of the characters is measured. Heathcliff is "a fierce, pitiless, wolfish man" (117), while Edgar Linton is a "sucking leveret" (131), and Linton Heathcliff is a "puling chicken" (237). Such figures are more than simple metaphors. They tell us that man in *Wuthering Heights*, as in the essay on the butterfly, is part of nature, and no different from other animals. Critics have commented on the prevalence of verbs of violent action in *Wuthering Heights*, verbs like "writhe, drag, crush, grind, struggle, yield, sink, recoil, outstrip, tear, drive asunder."[15] No other Victorian novel contains such scenes of inhuman brutality. No other novel so completely defines its characters in terms of the violence of their wills. In *Wuthering Heights*, people go on living only if their wills remain powerful and direct, capable of action so immediate and unthinking that it can hardly be called the result of choice, but is a permanent and unceasing attitude of aggression. Continuation of life for such people depends on their continuing to will, for in this world destruction is the law of life. If such characters cease to will, or if their wills weaken, motion slows, things coagulate, time almost stops, and their lives begin to weaken and fade away. Unless they can find some way to recuperate their wills, their lives will cease altogether, or tend slowly in the direction of death. So Lockwood, after his terrifying dreams, says, as the hours crawl toward morning, ". . . time stagnates here" (30). So the second Catherine, at the low point of her life, when only her own action will save her, says, "Oh! I'm tired—I'm *stalled* . . ." (342). And so Isabella, one of the weak people in the novel, can only escape from the tyranny of Heathcliff by precipitating herself into the realm of violence inhabited by the other characters who survive. The description of her escape from Wuthering Heights is a condensed distillation of the quality of life in the novel: "In my flight through the kitchen I bid Joseph speed to his master; I knocked over Hareton, who was hanging a litter of puppies from a chairback in the doorway; and, blest as a soul escaped from purgatory, I bounded, leaped, and flew down the steep road: then, quitting its windings, shot direct across the moor, rolling over banks, and wading through marshes; precipitating myself, in fact, towards the beacon light of the Grange" (208).

Lockwood learns when he makes his second visit to Wuthering Heights what it means to say that the people there live like ferocious dogs, and can survive only through the strength of their wills. He finds that everyone at the Heights hates everyone else with a violence of unrestrained rage which is like that of wild animals. Anarchy prevails. Even that mild Christian, Nelly Dean, accepts this universal selfishness when she says, "Well, we *must* be for ourselves in the long run; the mild and generous are only more justly selfish than the domineering . . ." (105). At Wuthering Heights only force is recognized as an intermediary between people, and each person follows as well as he can his own whim. "I'll put my trash away," says Catherine Linton to Heathcliff, "because you can make me, if I refuse . . . But I'll not do anything, though you should swear your tongue out, except what I please!" (33). As in Lockwood's dream of Jabes Branderham's sermon, every moral or religious law has disappeared, or has been transformed into an instrument of aggression. The "pilgrim's staves" of the church congregation are changed, in Lockwood's dream, into war clubs, and the service, which should be the model of a peaceful community, collectively submitting to divine law, becomes a scene of savage violence, recalling the two times when Lockwood has been attacked by dogs, and giving an accurate dream projection of the relations among the inmates of Wuthering Heights (26).

This animality of the people at the Heights is caused by the loss of an earlier state of civilized restraint. For a human being to act like an animal means something very different from a similar action performed by the animal itself. There are no laws for an animal to break, and there is nothing immoral in the slaughter of one animal by another. The characters in *Wuthering Heights* have *returned* to an animal state. Such a return is reached only through the transgression of all human law. The inmates of Wuthering Heights have destroyed the meaning of the word "moral," so that it can be used, as Heathcliff uses it, to define the most inhuman acts of cruelty (174).

Notes

14. *Wuthering Heights*, "The Shakespeare Head Brontë" (Boston and New York, 1931), p. 3. Numbers in parentheses after texts refer to page numbers in this edition.

15. Mark Schorer's list. See his introduction to the Rinehart edition of *Wuthering Heights* (New York, 1950), p. xv.

I would first like to clear out of the way the *confusions* of the plot and note the different levels on which the novel operates at different times. It seems clear to me that Emily Brontë had some trouble in getting free of a false start—a start which suggests that we are going to have a regional version of the sub-plot of *Lear* (Shakespeare being generally the inspiration for those early nineteenth-century novelists who rejected the eighteenth-century idea of the novel). In fact, the Lear-world of violence, cruelty, unnatural crimes, family disruption and physical horrors remains the world of the household at Wuthering Heights; a characteristic due not to sadism or perversion in the novelist (some of the physical violence is quite unrealized)[1] but to the Shakespearian intention. The troubles of the Earnshaws started when the father brought home the boy Heathcliff (of which he gives an unconvincing explanation and for whom he shows an unaccountable weakness) and forced him on the protesting family; Heathcliff 'the cuckoo' by intrigue soon ousts the legitimate son Hindley and, like Edmund, Gloucester's natural son in *Lear*, his malice brings about the ruin of two families (the Earnshaws and the Lintons, his rival getting the name Edgar by attraction from *Lear*). Clearly, Heathcliff was originally the illegitimate son and Catherine's half-brother, which would explain why, though so attached to him by early associations and natural sympathies, Catherine never really thinks of him as a possible lover either before or after marriage;[2] it also explains why all the children slept in one bed at the Heights till adolescence, we gather (we learn later from Catherine (Chapter XII) that being removed at puberty from this bed became a turning-point in her inner life, and this is only one of the remarkable insights which *Wuthering Heights* adds to the Romantic poets' exploration of childhood experience). The favourite Romantic theme of incest therefore must have been the impulsion behind the earliest conception of *Wuthering Heights*. Rejecting this story for a more mature intention, Emily Brontë was left with hopeless inconsistencies

46

on her hands, for while Catherine's feelings about Heathcliff are never sexual (though she feels the bond of sympathy with a brother to be more important to her than her feelings for her young husband), Heathcliff's feelings for her are always those of a lover. As Heathcliff has been written out as a half-brother, Catherine's innocent refusal to see that there is anything in her relation to him incompatible with her position as a wife, becomes preposterous and the impropriety which she refuses to recognize is translated into social terms—Edgar thinks the kitchen the suitable place for Heathcliff's reception by Mrs. Linton while she insists on the parlour. Another trace of the immature draft of the novel is the fairy-tale opening of the Earnshaw story, where the father, like the merchant in *Beauty and the Beast*, goes off to the city promising to bring his children back the presents each has commanded: but the fiddle was smashed and the whip lost so the only present he brings for them is the Beast himself, really a 'prince in disguise' (as Nelly tells the boy he should consider himself rightly); Catherine's tragedy then was that she forgot her prince and he was forced to remain the monster, destroying her; invoking this pattern brought in much more from the fairy-tale world of magic, folklore and ballads, the oral tradition of the folk, that the Brontë children learnt principally from their nurses and their servant Tabby.[3] This element surges up in Chapter XII, the important scene of Catherine's illness, where the dark superstitions about premonitions of death, about ghosts and primitive beliefs about the soul, come into play so significantly;[4] and again in the excessive attention given to Heathcliff's goblin-characteristics and especially to the prolonged account of his uncanny obsession and death. That this last should have an air of being infected by Hoffmann too is not surprising in a contemporary of Poe's; Emily is likely to have read Hoffmann when studying German at the Brussels boarding-school and certainly read the ghastly supernatural stories by James Hogg and others in the magazines at home. It is a proof of her immaturity at the time of the original conception of *Wuthering Heights* that she should express real psychological insights in such inappropriate forms.

In the novel as we read it Heathcliff's part either as Edmund in *Lear* or as the Prince doomed to Beast's form, is now suspended in boyhood while another influence, very much of the period, is developed, the Romantic image of childhood,[5] with a corresponding change of tone. Heathcliff and Catherine are idyllically and innocently happy together (and see also the end of Chapter V) roaming the countryside as hardy, primitive Wordsworthian children, 'half savage and hardy and free'. Catherine recalls it longingly when she feels she is dying trapped in Thrushcross Grange. (This boy Heathcliff is of course not assimilable with the vicious, scheming and morally heartless—'simply insensible'—boy of Chapter IV who plays Edmund to old Earnshaw's Gloucester.) Catherine's dramatic introduction to the genteel world of Thrushcross Grange—narrated with contempt by Heathcliff who is rejected by it as a plough-boy unfit to associate with Catherine—is the turning-point in her life in *this* form of the novel; her return, got up as a young lady in absurdly unsuitable clothes for a farmhouse life, and 'displaying fingers wonderfully whitened with doing nothing and staying indoors'[6] etc. visibly separates her from the 'natural' life, as her inward succumbing to the temptations of social superiority and riches parts her from Heathcliff.

Notes

1. *v.* Appendix B.

2. The speech (Chap. IX) in which Catherine explains to Nelly why she couldn't marry Heathcliff—on social grounds—belongs to the sociological *Wuthering Heights*. But even then she intends, she declares, to keep up her old (sisterly) relations with him, to help him get on in the world—'to *rise*' as she significantly puts it in purely social terms.

3. Tabby had, Mrs. Gaskell reports, 'known the "bottom" or valley in those primitive days when the faeries frequented the margin of the "beck" on moonlight nights, and had known folk who had seen them. But that was when there were no mills in the valleys, and when all the wool-spinning was done by hand in the farm-houses round. "It wur the factories as had driven 'em away", she said.'

4. *v.* Appendix C.

5. I am referring to the invaluable book, *The Image of Childhood*, by P. Coveney, though this does not in fact deal with *Wuthering Heights*.

6. This very evident judgment of Nelly's on the gentility with which Catherine has been infected by her stay at Thrushcross Grange (lavishly annotated in the whole scene of her return home in Chap. VII) is clearly endorsed by the author, since it is based on values that are fundamental to the novel and in consonance with Emily's Wordsworthian sympathies. It is supplemented by another similar but even more radical judgment, put into old Joseph's mouth, the indispensable Joseph who survives the whole action to go on farming the Heights and who is made the vehicle of several central judgments, as well as of many disagreeable Calvinistic attitudes. Resenting the boy Linton Heathcliff's contempt for the staple food, porridge, made, like the oat-cake, from the home-grown oats, Joseph remembers the boy's fine-lady mother: 'His mother were just soa—we wer a'most too mucky tuh sow t'corn fur makking her breead.' There are many related judgments in the novel. We may note here the near-caricature of Lockwood in the first three chapters as the town visitor continually exposing his ignorance of country life and farming.

U.C. Knoepflmacher on Lockwood's Unreliability

Emily Brontë knew that her bent, like Charlotte's, was romance; yet she was also astute enough to recognize that the dominant mode of the English novel was comic. Byron, who had written "Childe Harold" and *Manfred*, had also composed the comic *Don Juan*; Shakespeare, whose *King Lear* Lockwood remembers so incongruously when he is beset by Heathcliff's dogs, had blended humor and melodrama, laughter and terror. Emily's dramatic powers allowed her to control the fantasy world she had once shared with her brother and sisters. Her inventiveness allowed her to devise a framework in which the outer veneer of social comedy encases the truths of fantasy and myth.

In *Vanity Fair*, as we have seen, Thackeray was able to express his pessimistic outlook within the traditional framework of the comic novel by throwing out the dictionary definitions of good and evil and thereby forcing the reader to reassess reality itself. Though sharing this aim, Emily Brontë is far more radical in her departures. Thackeray's Showman refuses to act as our moral guide; yet his equivocations help to establish definable attitudes in the reader. The guide provided to the reader in the opening pages of *Wuthering Heights* proves to be totally unreliable. We cross the threshold of Heathcliff's mansion together with Lockwood only to find that the assumptions we have shared with this city man become totally untenable. Lockwood is a refugee from civilized society. His witty tone and extreme self-consciousness make him a distinct cousin of the jesting misanthropist who acts as Thackeray's narrator. Yet this Thackerayan figure, whose manners are urbane and whose outlook is comic, cannot cope with the asocial world he finds beyond the "threshold" of Wuthering Heights. His education becomes the reader's own, although, eventually, our understanding will surpass his.

Once inside the mansion Lockwood commits one blunder after another. Each overture, each phrase that he utters, results in a new misconception. In desperation, Lockwood cries out to the girl he has twice misidentified: "I want you to *tell* me my way, not to *show* it" (ch. 2). He demands to be led back to the sanity of Thrushcross Grange. After Lockwood is imprisoned by the snowstorm, the guide he demands will appear to him in a nightmare. Although the disturbing dream which he defends himself against was intended for Heathcliff—whose sensibilities are totally unlike his own, despite Lockwood's earlier, jocular identification of his host—the dream, though not telling Lockwood the way out of the labyrinth he has entered, begins to show us a new way of creating order. Lockwood, however, bound by his ordinary perceptions, fails to see that the creature outside the window is, potentially, a guide whose call for pity can rescue him from the "sin no Christian need pardon." Next day he relies on Heathcliff to conduct him back to the Grange. The snow-covered landscape has become treacherous: a "billowy, white ocean" has erased all landmarks, covering "rises and depressions in the ground: many pits, at least, were filled to a level" (ch. 3). Heathcliff follows stones erected to "serve as guides in the dark"; he warns the stumbling Lockwood to "steer to the right or left, when I imagined I was following, correctly, the winding of the road." Just as the external topography has altered from what "yesterday's walk left pictured" in Lockwood's mind, so has his neatly ordered inner world been disrupted by contradictions he has yet to sort out. Heathcliff stops at the gate of the Grange. Within its confines the exhausted Lockwood yields to a new "guide," Nelly Dean. Yet even her more sedate attempts to impose order and sanity on the reality he has experienced prove to be insufficient.

The reader is lured with Lockwood into the irrational world of *Wuthering Heights*. Like Lockwood, we have had barely time to take note of the lavish engravings on the front door, the date "1500," and the name "Hareton Earnshaw" before we are faced with incongruities we must decipher. The Heights lacks any "introductory lobby or passage," just as Emily Brontë's novel lacks the introductory passages furnished by a Trollope or Thackeray. Lockwood's initial experience is our own. As we stand on the threshold with him we too ponder between "speedy entrance" or "complete departure." On crossing the threshold we are mystified. Unsure of the causes for our mystification, we, like Lockwood, make the mistake of being overconfident. Soon, however, we are on the defensive. Our instinctive reaction is to flee, to be told the way out. Emily Brontë's Victorian readers took this way out. Confused by the discrepancy between Lockwood's polite diction and the atmosphere into which he is thrust, they must have been as confused as he is to find that a lady's furry "favourites" turn out to be a heap of dead rabbits. Yet the modern reader, more attuned to incongruity, gradually accepts the challenge. Whereas Lockwood represses the meaning of the two dreams he has experienced, we are willing to analyze their content. While Lockwood is content to lie on his back for most of the novel, willing to be entertained by Nelly's account, we continue to wander through a maze of conflicting attitudes, shifts in point of view, and abrupt changes in tone.

For a long while the reader is thwarted. Expectations misfire. Doors that seem open are shut; gates that seem closed turn out to provide us with an unexpected means of passage. Hovering between comic realism and the exaggerations of melodrama, this novel constantly avoids either extreme. In Thackeray's scheme, too, satire and sentiment qualify each other. But in *Wuthering Heights* these two modes merge and interpenetrate. Unlike *Vanity Fair*, Emily Brontë's novel moves toward a resolution. The social-comical realism of Lockwood and Nelly clashes with the asocial tragic myth enacted by Cathy and Heathcliff, but a new comic mode—represented by the idyll of the second Cathy and Hareton—bridges the chasm and ultimately provides the passage that seemed so impossible to find. In the novel's closing scene, Lockwood flees through the back door of the Heights. The reader, however, is rewarded for his endurance. He welcomes the restoration of order, and he wonders, with the departing Lockwood, how anarchy could ever have disrupted the benign face of "that quiet earth" (ch. 34). . . .

By her willingness to interpenetrate opposites, Emily Brontë achieves artistically what Catherine Earnshaw was unable to do. Catherine wanted to retain Edgar and Heathcliff, to live suspended between responsibility and freedom, civilization and eros, Victorian acquiescence and Romantic rebellion. Finding herself unable to span Edgar's social order and the life of instinct that she shared with Heathcliff, Cathy chooses to die, hoping to transcend a finite world of irreconcilables. The suspension she despairs of, however, is made possible by the novelist's construction of a form which encompasses these same alternatives. *Wuthering Heights* relies on the resemblances between opposites and the disjunction of alikes. Opposites blend: the Heathcliff who oppresses Hindley's son eventually matches the Hindley who oppressed Heathcliff; victim and tyrant become alike. Similarities are sundered: the Catherine who vows that she *is* Heathcliff survives, yet becomes altered, in the Linton daughter hated by Heathcliff. Only Joseph, oblivious to paradox and contradiction, always remains himself, unswerving in his self-righteousness, as eager to depreciate Heathcliff in the eyes of Hindley as he is to depreciate Hindley's son in the eyes of his new master. Joseph the fanatic, sure of his point of view, is an anomaly in Brontë's world.

CAROL JACOBS ON *WUTHERING HEIGHTS* AS METAFICTION

Like the entrance to Wonderland, the entrance to *Wuthering Heights* is marked by the metaphor of the doorway. Passage through that threshold will generate a crisis both in the voice of the self and in the logic of the good text. As in Carroll's text, where the adventures in Wonderland ultimately fall under the aegis of the dream, so in *Wuthering Heights* one dreams of finding its center only to find that the center is a dream.

We enter *Wuthering Heights* through the voice of Lockwood, who devotes the first three chapters of his narrative to what he twice calls the "repetition of my intrusion." These intrusions are, to be sure, the literal incursions he makes into the house of Wuthering Heights but they function no less as attempts to penetrate *Wuthering Heights-as-text.* The outsider, conventional in language as well as understanding, makes repeated efforts to force his way to the penetralium. Yet one knocks vainly for admittance at these locked doors and, on his second visit, the intruder enters only by means of a violence which almost matches that of Wuthering Heights itself. He penetrates to the innermost chamber of the structure and to the enclosed oaken bed within, and here he experiences the very center of Wuthering Heights as a dream, or, more accurately, as a series of nightmares. This dream-troubled night rapidly results in Lockwood's excommunication from Wuthering Heights, for the illness brought on by these events confines him to Thrushcross Grange. At the same juncture, Nelly Dean replaces Lockwood in his role as narrator, for Lockwood becomes the mere recorder of Nelly's story.

How are we to interpret this curious point of articulation between the first three chapters of the novel and the narrative that follows? Certainly not by taking Lockwood at his word. He organizes his explanation by suppressing all further mention of the dreams and by linking the subsequent events into a simplistic causal chain. A sleepless night and a difficult journey through the snow bring on a bad cold. The illness, in turn, incapacitates him, and so he calls in the housekeeper to entertain him with her tales. A fiction surely, for if we return to Chapter III, we find that the texts of the dream dislocate the possibility of such explanation. The exclusion of Lockwood from the Heights and the displacement of Lockwood as direct narrator of the novel, his excommunication from Wuthering Heights both as a banishment from its community and as a relegation to a position outside of communication, are already the common, if oblique, themes of the dreams themselves. They mark the disjunction not only between Lockwood and Wuthering Heights but also between Lockwood and *Wuthering Heights-as-text*. For these passages offer a commentary on the nature of the fictional space marked off as Nelly's narrative, a commentary which is made possible by setting off Lockwood as that which lies outside the fictional realm. The exact locus of this commentary will remain equivocal; for it lies somewhere between Lockwood's puzzlement and Nelly's explanation, and yet again at the heart of *Wuthering Heights*.

Finally closeted within the panelled bed, Lockwood imagines he had delineated a protective boundary between himself and the threatening realm without: "I slid back the panelled sides, got in with my light, pulled them together again, and felt secure against the vigilance of Heathcliff, and every one else" (WH, 25). The diary records but two descriptive details of this apparently secure inner space: "a few mildewed books" lie piled in the corner of the window ledge, and the ledge itself is "covered with writing scratched on the paint" (WH, 25). Having reached the very center of Wuthering Heights, Lockwood finds it inhabited by texts. And not just any texts. For the scratchings of Catherine and the books of her library, whose margins also contain her diary, figure most significantly in Lockwood's dreams. Each dream incorporates one of these three texts. In the first appear the spectre-like letters etched on the sill. The second concerns the pious discourse of Jabes Branderham, which Lockwood had just begun reading. The third personifies the child Cathy, who speaks from the pages of her diary.

Lockwood's narrative elaborates a system of "careful causality" to establish the relationship between text and dream.

He describes himself reading Catherine's name and then dreaming of it. He wakes to find his candle burning one of the good books, and so peruses them. He dreams once again of the text he has just been reading and is awakened by "a shower of loud taps on the boards of the pulpit, which responded so smartly that, at last, to my unspeakable relief, they woke me" (WH, 29). He locates the dream-source in the title of Jabes's sermon, and its noisy conclusion is easily explained away by assigning it to a referent in the "real world," the branch of the fir tree: "And what was it that had suggested the tremendous tumult, what had played Jabes's part in the row? Merely the branch of a fir tree that touched my lattice, as the blast wailed by, and rattled its dry cones against the panes!" (WH, 29). Lockwood attributes his last dream to the reading of Cathy's diary: "'The truth is, sir, I passed the first part of the night in—' here, I stopped afresh—I was about to say 'perusing those old volumes;' then it would have revealed my knowledge of their written, as well as their printed contents . . ." (WH, 32).

Lockwood interprets his dreams by rooting them firmly in his waking world. In this manner he attempts to establish the ascendancy of reality over dream and to dispense with a merely fictional terror by rational explication. Yet the terror of fiction is otherwise. The "reality" by means of which Lockwood claims deliverance is, after all, rather a series of texts. And looking to the dreams themselves, we find they give those texts quite another interpretation. In each of the dreams, the dreamer is engaged in a violent struggle and it is precisely those apparently innocuous texts which function as his vicious adversaries.

The waking Lockwood imagines himself victorious in these conflicts, but the dreams themselves tell the story of a different mastery. First, the glaring letters of Catherine's name swarm at Lockwood; then it is quite literally the text of Jabes Branderham's sermon which assaults him; and, finally, he struggles unsuccessfully with a figure arisen from Cathy's diary, or "an impression which personified itself . . ." (WH, 32) out of the name Catherine Linton.

In his second dream, Lockwood is condemned to endure the endless sermon of Jabes Branderham. With each division of the sermon, Lockwood rises to go, but is forced each time to resume his seat:

> Oh, how weary I grew. How I writhed, and yawned, and nodded, and revived! How I pinched and pricked myself, and rubbed my eyes, and stood up, and sat down again, and nudged Joseph to inform me if he would *ever* have done!
> I was condemned to hear all out. . . . (WH, 29)

The forgiveness demanded of Lockwood strangely figures as forgiveness of the discourse itself rather than of the sins the text names. The length of the text and especially the repetitive nature of its structure make its textuality more prevalent than its content:

> "Sir," I exclaimed, "sitting here, within these four walls, at one stretch, I have endured and forgiven the four hundred and ninety heads of your discourse. Seventy times seven times have I plucked up my hat and been about to depart—Seventy times seven times have you preposterously forced me to resume my seat. The four hundred and ninety-first is too much." (WH, 29)

The four hundred and ninety-first attempt to deny the text, this time by destroying Jabes Branderham, the refusal to forgive the four hundred and ninety-first head of the discourse is the sin for which Lockwood cannot be forgiven. As anticipated, the sentence of excommunication is handed down:

> "*Thou art the Man!*" cried Jabes, after a solemn pause, leaning over his cushion. "Seventy times seven times didst thou gapingly contort they visage—seventy times seven did I take counsel with my soul—Lo, this is human weakness; this also may be absolved! The First of the Seventy-First is come. Brethren, execute upon him the judgment written! such honour have all His saints!"

With that concluding word, the whole assembly, exalting their pilgrim's staves, rushed round me in a body. . . . (WH, 29)

Although its violence is initially masked, it is ultimately the endless text which wields the power to destroy Lockwood.

Sandra M. Gilbert and Susan Gubar on *Wuthering Heights* and Milton's Satan

Milton, Winifred Gérin tells us, was one of Patrick Brontë's favorite writers, so if Shelley was Milton's critic's daughter, Brontë was Milton's admirer's daughter.[6] By the Hegelian law of thesis/antithesis, then, it seems appropriate that Shelley chose to repeat and restate Milton's misogynistic story while Brontë chose to correct it. In fact the most serious matter *Wuthering Heights* and *Frankenstein* share is the matter of *Paradise Lost*, and their profoundest difference is in their attitude toward Milton's myth. Where Shelley was Milton's dutiful daughter, retelling his story to clarify it, Brontë was the poet's rebellious child, radically revising (and even reversing) the terms of his mythic narrative. Given the fact that Brontë never mentions either Milton or *Paradise Lost* in *Wuthering Heights*, any identification of her as Milton's daughter may at first seem eccentric or perverse. Shelley, after all, provided an overtly Miltonic framework in *Frankenstein* to reinforce our sense of her literary intentions. But despite the absence of Milton references, it eventually becomes plain that *Wuthering Heights* is also a novel haunted by Milton's bogey. We may speculate, indeed, that Milton's absence is itself a presence, so painfully does Brontë's story dwell on the places and persons of his imagination.

That *Wuthering Heights* is about heaven and hell, for instance, has long been seen by critics, partly because all the narrative voices, from the beginning of Lockwood's first visit to the Heights, insist upon casting both action and description in religious terms, and partly because one of the first Catherine's major speeches to Nelly Dean raises the questions "What is heaven? Where is hell?" perhaps more urgently than any other speech in an English novel:

> "If I were in heaven, Nelly, I should be extremely miserable. . . . I dreamt once that I was there [and] that heaven did not seem to be my home, and I broke my heart with weeping to come back to earth; and the angels were so angry that they flung me out into the middle of the heath on the top of Wuthering Heights, where I woke sobbing for joy."[7]

Satan too, however—at least Satan as Milton's prototypical Byronic hero—has long been considered a participant in *Wuthering Heights*, for "that devil Heathcliff," as both demon lover and ferocious natural force, is a phenomenon critics have always studied. Isabella's "Is Mr. Heathcliff a man? If so, is he mad? And if not is he a devil?" (chap. 13) summarizes the traditional Heathcliff problem most succinctly, but Nelly's "I was inclined to believe . . . that conscience had turned his heart to an earthly hell" (chap. 33) more obviously echoes *Paradise Lost*.

Again, that *Wuthering Heights* is in some sense about a fall has frequently been suggested, though critics from Charlotte Brontë to Mark Schorer, Q. D. Leavis, and Leo Bersani have always disputed its exact nature and moral implications. Is Catherine's fall the archetypal fall of the *Bildungsroman* protagonist? Is Heathcliff's fall, his perverted "moral teething," a shadow of Catherine's? Which of the two worlds of *Wuthering Heights* (if either) does Brontë mean to represent the truly "fallen" world? These are just some of the controversies that have traditionally attended this issue. Nevertheless, that the story of *Wuthering Heights* is built around a central fall seems indisputable, so that a description of the novel as in part a *Bildungsroman* about a girl's passage from "innocence" to "experience" (leaving aside the precise meaning of those terms) would probably also be widely accepted. And that the fall in *Wuthering Heights* has Miltonic overtones is no doubt culturally inevitable. But even if it weren't, the Miltonic implications of the action would be clear enough from the "mad scene" in which Catherine describes herself as "an exile, and outcast . . . from what had been my world," adding "Why am I so changed? Why does my blood rush into a hell of tumult at a few words?" (chap. 12). Given the metaphysical nature of *Wuthering Heights*, Catherine's definition of herself as "an exile and outcast" inevitably suggests those trail-blazing exiles and outcasts Adam, Eve, and Satan. And her Romantic question—"Why am I so changed?"—with its desperate straining after the roots of identity, must ultimately refer back to Satan's hesitant (but equally crucial) speech to Beelzebub, as they lie stunned in the lake of fire: "If thou be'est he; But O . . . how chang'd" (*PL* l. 84).

Of course, *Wuthering Heights* has often, also, been seen as a subversively visionary novel. Indeed, Brontë is frequently coupled with Blake as a practitioner of mystical politics. Usually, however, as if her book were written to illustrate the enigmatic religion of "No coward soul is mine," this visionary quality is related to Catherine's assertion that she is tired of "being enclosed" in "this shattered prison" of her body, and "wearying to escape into that glorious world, and to be always there" (chap. 15). Many readers define Brontë, in other words, as a ferocious pantheist/transcendentalist, worshipping the manifestations of the One in rock, tree, cloud, man and woman, while manipulating her story to bring about a Romantic *Liebestod* in which favored characters enter "the endless and shadowless hereafter." And certainly such ideas, like Blake's *Songs of Innocence*, are "something heterodox," to use Lockwood's phrase. At the same time, however, they are soothingly rather than disquietingly neo-Miltonic, like fictionalized visions of *Paradise Lost*'s luminous Father God. They are, in fact, the ideas of "steady, reasonable" Nelly Dean, whose denial of the demonic in life, along with her commitment to the angelic tranquility of death, represents only one of the visionary alternatives in *Wuthering Heights*. And, like Blake's metaphor of the lamb, Nelly's pious alternative has no real meaning for Brontë outside of the context provided by its tigerish opposite.

The tigerish opposite implied by *Wuthering Heights* emerges most dramatically when we bring all the novel's Miltonic elements together with its author's personal concerns in an attempt at a single formulation of Brontë's metaphysical intentions: the sum of this novel's visionary parts is an almost shocking revisionary whole. Heaven (or its rejection), hell, Satan, a fall, mystical politics, metaphysical romance, orphanhood, and the question of origins—disparate as some of these matters may seem, they all cohere in a rebelliously topsy-turvy retelling of Milton's and Western culture's central tale of the fall of woman and her shadow self, Satan. This fall, says Brontë, is not a fall *into* hell. It is a fall *from* "hell" into "heaven," not a fall from grace (in the religious sense) but a fall into grace (in the cultural sense). Moreover, for the heroine who falls it is the loss of Satan rather than the loss of God that signals the painful passage from innocence to experience. Emily Brontë, in other words, is not just Blakeian in "double" mystical vision, but Blakeian in a tough, radically political commitment to the belief that the state of being patriarchal Christianity calls "hell" is eternally, energetically delightful, whereas the state called "heaven" is rigidly hierarchical, Urizenic, and "kind" as a poison tree. But because she was metaphorically one of Milton's daughters, Brontë differs from Blake, that powerful son of a powerful father, in reversing the terms of Milton's Christian cosmogony for specifically feminist reasons.

Notes

6. Gérin, *Emily Brontë*, p. 47.

7. Norton Critical Edition of *Wuthering Heights*, p. 72. All references will be to this edition.

Patsy Stoneman on "Romantic" Love

The English Romantic poets were the 'modern' writers of Emily Brontë's youth; she almost certainly knew about their sensational lives and deaths, and read their works in editions published during her teens. Shelley's poem, 'Epipsychidion', has in particular been recognized as relevant to *Wuthering Heights*.[7] Its title seems to mean 'song for the soul outside the soul', and thus matches closely Catherine Earnshaw's conviction that 'there is or should be an existence of yours beyond you'. Shelley feels such oneness with his 'other soul' (Emilia Viviani) that he exclaims, 'Ah me! I am not thine: I am a part of *thee*',[8] just as Catherine tells Nelly, 'Whatever our souls are made of, his and mine are the same ... Nelly, I *am* Heathcliff' (pp. 100–2). It is significant that when Percy Shelley wrote 'Epipsychidion', Emilia (also called Emily) was confined to a convent, so that their union was unlikely; this kind of 'Romantic love' (which I shall give a capital letter to distinguish it from the kind that leads to marriage) derives its intensity precisely from unfulfilled desire. ...

Shelley extols spiritual oneness in the 'aspiring' terms typical of the male Romantics:

We shall become the same, we shall be one ...
In one another's substance finding food,
Like flames too pure and light and unimbued
To nourish their bright lives with baser prey,
Which point to Heaven and cannot pass away:
One hope within two wills, one will beneath
Two overshadowing minds, one life, one death,
One Heaven, one Hell, one immortality,
And one annihilation. Woe is me!
The winged words on which my soul would pierce
Into the height of Love's rare Universe,
Are chains of lead around its flight of fire—
I pant, I sink, I tremble, I expire! (lines 573–91)

Heathcliff's exhumation of Catherine's corpse deflates Shelley's airy rhetoric with the physical reality of death and Catherine and Heathcliff both look for 'the height of Love's rare Universe' in or on the earth;[11] nevertheless Emily Brontë's novel is widely read as an instance of Shelleyan mirror-like Romantic love.[12]

If we accept the distinction outlined above between 'romantic' and 'Romantic' love, then logically there ought to be two constituencies of readers, wishing for one of two outcomes: either that Catherine should have married Heathcliff instead of Edgar (romantic love); or that Catherine should have preserved a spiritual affinity with Heathcliff by not marrying anybody (Romantic love). Yet readers regularly (if unconsciously) amalgamate these positions, finding in the notion of reunion after death a promise of consummation whose nature remains unspecific. We want, it seems, not to choose between options, but to imagine lovers who are at once transcendent and embodied.

What seems beyond dispute is that Catherine's marriage to Edgar provides the tragic machinery which precludes earthly fulfilment for her and Heathcliff. Strictly, Catherine and Heathcliff's relationship is negated by Catherine and Edgar's only if we see it as 'romantic' (marriage-orientated) love; as 'Romantic' (mirror-like) love it is merely different. But because our social conventions endorse only exclusive relationships between adult men and women, it seems inevitable that we cast the story in terms of a competition between Heathcliff and Edgar. In this competition, Edgar has the advantage of legitimacy, but because our pervasive value-system ranks 'soul' more highly than 'body', the 'sublime' love of Catherine and Heathcliff is nevertheless generally preferred.[13] Most critics endorse Heathcliff's judgement that, in marrying Edgar, Catherine has 'betray[ed her] own heart' (p. 198).[14] What I want to suggest is that, far from self-betrayal, Catherine attempts a fulfilment so comprehensive as to be uncomprehended by the other characters in the novel and by her readers.

It is true that Catherine tells Nelly that 'in my soul, and in my heart, I'm convinced I'm wrong!' in intending to marry Edgar (p. 98) and her words here are famous: 'Whatever our souls are made of [Heathcliff's] and mine are the same, and Linton's is as different as a moonbeam from lightning, or frost from fire' (p. 100). What follows, however, has had less critical attention. When Nelly asks how she thinks Heathcliff will bear the separation, Catherine is amazed: 'Who is to separate us, pray? . . . Oh, that's not what I intend—that's not what I mean!' (p. 101). This strange speech has provoked some readers into asking exactly what she *does* mean. Q. D. Leavis can only explain it by supposing that in some original plan for the novel, Heathcliff was to be Catherine's half-brother, which would clearly rule out their marriage, while making it natural for them to be together. For Leavis, 'Catherine's innocent refusal to see that there is anything in her relation to [Heathcliff] incompatible with her position as a wife, becomes preposterous' when their kinship is 'written out' of the finished novel.[15]

Nevertheless, Catherine persists in her 'preposterous' assumptions. When Heathcliff returns to find her married to Edgar, she is delirious with joy. No sense of tragic irony seems to enter into her consciousness, nor any foreboding of difficulties. After she asked Nelly who was to separate her from Heathcliff, Catherine had continued, 'I shouldn't be Mrs. Linton were such a price demanded! He'll be as much to me as he has been all his lifetime. Edgar must shake off his antipathy, and tolerate him, at least' (p. 101). Now she acts on this assumption, telling Edgar that 'for my sake, you must be friends now', and trying to force the two men to shake hands (pp. 117–18). She continues in a state of high good humour until it becomes obvious that neither Heathcliff nor Edgar is willing to play their part in this triangular 'friendship'.

Catherine's behaviour here provokes epithets like 'preposterous' because she does not recognize that the code appropriate for children who shared a bed is inappropriate for a married woman and a male friend; and because she seems unconscious of impropriety, her love has been seen as sexless.[16] The text gives us no clue whether Catherine sees Heathcliff as a potential sexual partner; there is, however, a literary model for such a triangle which is less evasive. This is the very same poem that has been cited in evidence of the 'oneness' of two of the triangle. Shelley's 'Epipsychidion' is in fact much better known for its manifesto of free love than for its 'twin soul' theme:

I never was attached to that great sect,
Whose doctrine is, that each one should select
Out of the crowd a mistress or a friend,
And all the rest, though fair and wise, commend
To cold oblivion, though it is in the code
Of modern morals, and the beaten road
Which those poor slaves with weary footsteps tread,
Who travel to their home among the dead
By the broad highway of the world, and so
With one chained friend, perhaps a jealous foe,
The dreariest and the longest journey go.

True Love in this differs from gold and clay,
That to divide is not to take away.
Love is like understanding, that grows bright,
Gazing on many truths; 'tis like thy light,
Imagination! which from earth and sky,
And from the depths of human fantasy,
As from a thousand prisms and mirrors, fills
The Universe with glorious beams, and kills
Error, the worm, with many a sun-like arrow
Of its reverberated lightning. Narrow
The heart that loves, the brain that contemplates,
The life that wears, the spirit that creates
One object, and one form, and builds thereby
A sepulchre for its eternity. (lines 149–73)

Notes

7. See F. B. Pinion, *A Brontë Companion* (Basingstoke, 1975), 216 n.; W. Gérin, *Emily Brontë* (Oxford, 1978), 44–5, 153–4; E. Chitham, 'Emily Brontë and Shelley', *Brontë Society Transactions*, 17 (1978), 195; E. Chitham, *Emily Brontë* (Oxford, 1987), 73, 99, 133–4.

8. Percy Shelley, 'Epipsychidion', line 52. Shelley quotations are from *Poetical Works*, ed. T. Hutchinson (Oxford, 1967).

11. For accounts of Emily Brontë's 'literalizing' of Romantic spiritualities, see E. Moers, *Literary Women* (London, 1978); M. Homans, 'The Name of the Mother in *Wuthering Heights*', *Bearing the Word: Language and Female Experience in Nineteenth-century Women's Writing* (Chicago, 1986), 68–83; C. Senf, 'Emily Brontë's Version of

Feminist History: *Wuthering Heights*', *Essays in Literature*, 12 (1985), 204–14; S. Davies, *Emily Brontë* (Brighton, 1988).

12. Edward Chitham, for instance, uses the lines quoted above from 'Epipsychidion' as epigraph to his Introduction to *Emily Brontë*.

13. For similar reasons, the older Catherine and Heathcliff are preferred to the younger Catherine and Hareton and, in the twentieth century, *Wuthering Heights* has been regarded as a 'greater' novel than *Jane Eyre*.

14. e.g. Visick, *Genesis of Wuthering Heights*, 9; A. Kettle, *An Introduction to the English Novel* (London, 1951), i. 145.

15. Q. D. Leavis, 'A Fresh Approach to *Wuthering Heights*', *Lectures in America* (Cambridge, 1969), i. 232.

16. Leavis, 'A Fresh Approach', 232.

BERNARD J. PARIS ON HEATHCLIFF'S CHARACTER

Unlike most critics, I believe that Heathcliff and Cathy are imagined human beings whose behavior can be understood in motivational terms. One of the major questions in both the novel and the criticism is what kind of a being is Heathcliff. In the novel, the question is posed most directly by Isabella: "Is Mr. Heathcliff a man? If so, is he mad? And if not, is he a devil?" (ch. 13). When she flees from the Heights, Isabella calls him an "incarnate goblin" and a "monster" and wishes that "he could be blotted out of creation" (ch. 17). Nelly replies, "Hush, hush! He's a human being" and urges Isabella to "be more charitable." Nelly is the chief proponent of Heathcliff's human status. Watching his agony at the death of Catherine, she thinks, "Poor wretch! . . . you have a heart and nerves the same as your brother men!" (ch. 16). Near the end, however, even Nelly wonders if Heathcliff is "a ghoul, or a vampire" (ch. 34).

The issue for critics has not been whether Heathcliff is a ghoul or a human being, but whether he is a realistically drawn figure or some other kind of character about whom it is inappropriate to ask motivational questions. A common view has been that as a character in a Gothic romance, he is an archetype, symbol, or projection of the unconscious who is not supposed to be understood as though he were a person. I believe that Emily Brontë meant Heathcliff to be perceived as

65

a human being, since despite the aura of mystery with which she surrounds the question of his nature, she is at pains to make his behavior seem naturalistically motivated. As Frances Russell Hart observes, the Gothic represents not "a flight from novel to romance," but "a naturalizing of myth and romance into novel" (1968, 103). The central experience it offers is a "dreadful, sublime shock to one's complacently enlightened idea of human character and the reality to which it belongs" (88). In order for the Gothic to achieve this shock, its characters must be imagined human beings whose behavior, however strange, is psychologically credible.

Heathcliff retains his human status, however fiendlike he becomes, because Emily Brontë keeps telling us that he has been victimized and that his viciousness arises from his misery. Perhaps the strongest evidence that she meant us to see his cruelty as a natural phenomenon is the fact that several characters articulate the principle that bad treatment leads to vindictiveness, and several others illustrate its operation. Even the pampered, innocuous Linton girls turn savage after a brief exposure to Heathcliff. After her escape, Isabella lusts for revenge. Sounding much like Heathcliff, she wants to "take an eye for an eye, a tooth for a tooth; for every wrench of agony [to] return a wrench, [to] reduce him to my level" (ch. 17). And Nelly observes of the young Catherine that "the more hurt she gets, the more venomous she grows" (ch. 30). Abuse quickly generates powerful vindictive impulses in these girls, and their sufferings are trivial compared to what Heathcliff endured in childhood.

I believe that the failure to understand Heathcliff as a person has two main sources. The first is that many critics have entertained a view of the novel as predominantly metaphysical, lyric, or Gothic that has prevented them from even attempting to make sense of Heathcliff's behavior. The second is that Heathcliff's love for Cathy and his vindictiveness toward the Earnshaws and the Lintons have seemed so extreme as to be beyond the pale of human nature. Critics have deemed Heathcliff unrealistic, in effect, because his behavior has escaped their comprehension. There is always the possibility that the author's intuitive grasp of psychological phenomena is deeper than our conceptual understanding. We can recover Emily Brontë's intuitions, I believe, with the aid of Karen Horney, assisted by R. D. Laing and Abraham Maslow. Heathcliff's vindictiveness and devotion to Cathy are both intelligible as defensive reactions to the deprivation and abuse to which he was subjected in childhood.

According to Abraham Maslow (1970), all humans have a set of basic needs that must be reasonably well met if they are to develop in a healthy way. In the order of their potency, these are physiological survival needs, needs for safety, for love and belonging, for esteem, and for self-actualization. Frustration of the basic needs arrests development and leads individuals to develop defensive strategies for making up their deficiencies. If we consider Heathcliff's childhood with the basic needs in mind, it is evident that he was severely deprived. Mr. Earnshaw finds him at about the age of six "starving and houseless, and as good as dumb in the streets of Liverpool" (ch. 4). He appears to have been abandoned by his family and to have lost, or never fully acquired, the art of language. When Mr. Earnshaw picks him up, his very survival is in jeopardy. He has been living, for we know not how long, in a state that is radically devoid of safety, love and belonging, and esteem.

When Mr. Earnshaw brings him home, Heathcliff has a protector at last; but he meets with contempt and rejection from the other members of the household. Everyone refers to him as "it"; and Nelly, the children, and Mrs. Earnshaw would all like him to disappear. He gradually gains a place in the family, but it is never a secure one, and he is always an object of hostility. When Mr. Earnshaw dies, Heathcliff is entirely dependent on Hindley, who hates him. He has only one relationship that makes him feel secure, and that is with Cathy. It is no wonder that he clings to her with such intensity.

Heathcliff is a severely deprived, frequently abused child who develops all three of Horney's interpersonal strategies of defense. The very reserved Lockwood describes him as "a man who seemed more exaggeratedly reserved than myself" (ch. 1). In addition to his exaggerated withdrawal, Heathcliff displays extreme forms of aggression and compliance. All the suggestions of demonism, vampirism, and ghoulishness derive from his unrelenting vindictiveness and his sadistic delight in the suffering of his victims. His frantic dependency on Cathy is one of the most intense emotions in all of literature. It is so extreme that many critics feel it can be explained only in metaphysical terms. Unlike most of the people Horney describes, Heathcliff avoids inner conflict not by subordinating any of his trends, but by a process of compartmentalization. He moves toward Cathy, against Hindley and the Lintons, and away from everyone else.

Heathcliff's initial defense is detachment. When Mr. Earnshaw brings him to the Heights, he protects himself against the hostility he meets there by trying to be invulnerable: "He seemed a sullen, patient child," says Nelly, "hardened, perhaps, to ill-treatment: he would stand Hindley's blows without winking or shedding a tear, and my pinches moved him only to draw in a breath, and open his eyes as if he had hurt himself by accident, and nobody was to blame" (ch. 4). Heathcliff is showing them, in effect, that they cannot hurt him. His only way of gaining a sense of control in a hostile world is by not reacting to what is done to him. He follows the same pattern during his illness: whereas Cathy and Hindley harass Nelly terribly, Heathcliff is "as uncomplaining as a lamb, though hardness, not gentleness, made him give little trouble." He gives little trouble because he does not expect anyone to be concerned about him, and it is important for him to feel that he is not dependent on them.

Heathcliff practices a resignation to suffering that removes him from the power of other people and makes him impervious to the slings and arrows of outrageous fortune. He denies that anything is impinging on him and distances himself from his own feelings. Since he has no reason to trust other people or to expect anything but pain from his dealings with them, he is sullen, withdrawn, and unsociable. When his situation worsens after the death of Hindley's wife, "his naturally reserved disposition was exaggerated," says Nelly, "into an almost idiotic excess of unsociable moroseness" (ch. 8).

MARIANNE THORMÄHLEN ON CATHERINE'S SELF-OBSESSION

There is some thing decidedly odd about this supposedly archetypal romance. What truly infatuated teenage girl tells a confidante that marrying the boy from whom she claims to be inseparable would degrade her? What of Catherine's claim, uttered at the same time, to 'love the ground under [Edgar's] feet, and the air over his head, and everything he touches, and everything he says'? And how can two people supposedly in love torment each other so cruelly as Catherine and Heathcliff do, recklessly repeating unloverlike assertions such as 'I care nothing for your sufferings' and 'I have not one word of comfort—you deserve this'?

For anyone who turns his or her 'attention to the human core of the novel', as Q. D. Leavis urged *Wuthering Heights* critics to do,[3] a fundamental problem manifests itself: the problem of sympathy. The varying views regarding the relative degrees of evil exhibited by the characters in *Wuthering Heights* reflect the issue, from the early condemnations of Heathcliff to the twentieth-century attempts to assign the villain's role to Nelly Dean (or even Lockwood).[4] Nelly herself illustrates the difficulty: both Catherine[5] and Heathcliff treat her as a friend and confidante; but although she is capable of warmth, even devotion (as is apparent in her love of her two charges, Hareton and Cathy), she seems strangely unmoved by the sufferings of the two 'lovers' whom she has known since childhood. In fact, as James Hafsley and others have pointed out, her actions sometimes exacerbate them. As for Catherine and Heathcliff themselves, they have no tenderness or compassion for anybody, not even for each other.

'I own I did not like her, after her infancy was past.'[6] Nelly's frank admission prepares the reader for her seeming callousness in the face of young Mrs. Linton's troubles. Catherine Earnshaw never sets any store by being liked: during her father's decline, for example, she takes positive delight in harassing him, and 'she was never so happy as when we were all scolding her at once'.[7] Nor does she take much trouble to win the friendship of the Lintons, and she does not have to: the 'honeysuckle' of the Grange dwellers is always all too ready to wind itself around her 'thorn'.[8] Sure of Heathcliff's, and later Edgar's, unconditional devotion, she is basically uninterested in what anyone else might feel about her.

While the boy Heathcliff's wrongs at Hindley Earnshaw's hands at least foster a feeling that he is the victim of harshness and injustice, the growth of true sympathy for him is checked by several circumstances, such as his lack of discernible affection for his benefactor, old Mr. Earnshaw; the realization that Hindley has cause to be jealous, having had his nose cruelly put out of joint by the sudden arrival of the new favourite; Heathcliff's blackmailing effort over the colts; and his intractable sullenness, even to Catherine, during his years of degradation. It should be noted, though, that none of this prevents Nelly from pitying the young Heathcliff even to tears and from trying, unsuccessfully, to remedy his situation. It is when the grown man resorts to deception and cruelty against those whom she loves (and against herself, too) that Nelly gradually withdraws from Heathcliff, to the point of refusing to sit with him when he asks for someone to keep him company shortly before his death.

Fortunately, interest in a person is not dependent on sympathy for him or her, or Lockwood would never have asked the housekeeper at Thrushcross Grange to tell him 'the history of Mr. Heathcliff', and she could not have rendered such a detailed narrative, down to reproductions of lengthy conversations. The contrast between the humdrum narrators in *Wuthering Heights* and the extraordinary main protagonists of the story has been commented on for more than a hundred years. The failures and foibles of the former ensure that a reader's sympathy is not naturally driven to fuse with any viewpoint of theirs. The result is that the reader is liberated from any pressure to identify with any person or persons in the novel. Emily Brontë forces us to take up our own standpoint, or to decide to forgo the adoption of any point of view at all. There are several indications to the effect that this absence of guidance towards an attitude is the outcome of a deliberate authorial policy. Brontë does not even allow young Cathy—warmhearted and courageous in herself, but stubborn, spoilt, and inconsiderate, too—to ingratiate herself with the reader, any more than she does with Lockwood on his first arrival at the Heights.

The nature of the bond between Catherine and Heathcliff has been the subject of much speculation. Several recent commentators have picked up the suggestion, first put forward—as far as I have been able to find out—by Eric Solomon,[9] that Heathcliff may have been an illegitimate child of old Mr. Earnshaw's, and hence Catherine's half-brother. This would go some way towards accounting for the kinship one senses between them. In addition, it would explain Mr. Earnshaw's seemingly incomprehensible partiality for the gypsy-dark foundling. The chroniclers of Gondal and Angria, who were also admirers of Byron, were thoroughly familiar with the existence of various kinds of forbidden love, including that of half-siblings. The sexlessness of the Catherine–Heathcliff relationship, noted (as 'purity') by early reviewers and emphasized in Lord David Cecil's seminal appraisal,[10] has been regarded in the light of possible blood ties. But if Catherine and Heathcliff are indeed related by blood, they will hardly know it themselves. Nor will anybody else after the death of old Mr. Earnshaw, who does nothing to check their intimacy. Consequently, talk of 'incest' seems a little off-target.

The only time when the closeness between Catherine and Heathcliff is untroubled by anything except the interference of elders is their childhood. It is a state of total alliance which ends with Catherine's first stay at the Grange, from which she returns transformed into a young lady. Exposed to the attractions of luxury, refinement, and flattery (Frances Earnshaw adopts the latter strategy in her attempts to civilize her wayward sister-in-law), the pathologically egotistical Catherine Earnshaw begins to explore other avenues of self-gratification than the ones she shared with her childhood companion.

'Pathologically egotistical' is a drastic expression, but Catherine's self-obsession is always more potent than the ordinary self-centredness of the young. Not even Nelly's suggestion that the little girl means no real harm when deliberately vexing family and servants is unproblematic: 'when once she made you cry in good earnest, it seldom happened that she would not keep you company, and oblige you to be quiet that you might comfort her.'[11] In other words, she compels her victims to devote their sympathy to the author of their anger and pain. This hardly constitutes exculpatory behaviour in any human being, regardless of age.

It is Catherine's inability to regard her self and her conduct from a distance, and to admit the possibility of other views of reality than hers, that makes for her undoing and Heathcliff's. Not that she is totally insensitive to her surroundings; Nelly is amused by the 15-year-old girl's attempts to adapt herself to the company she happens to be in, acting in a ladylike manner among the Lintons and giving free rein to her 'unruly nature' at the Heights. Nelly is shrewd enough, though, to appreciate that Catherine evinces this 'double character without exactly intending to deceive anyone'.[12] In her self-absorption, it does not occur to the 'heroine' of *Wuthering Heights* that she cannot have, and be, everything she wants whenever she wants it.

Notes

3. Q.D. Leavis, 'A Fresh Approach to *Wuthering Heights*', from F.R. and Q.D. Leavis, *Lectures in America* (New York, 1969); quoted in the Norton Critical Edition of *Wuthering Heights*, ed. W. M. Sale, Jr. (New York, 1972), 321.

4. Several commentators have remarked that modern criticism of *Wuthering Heights* has tended to become increasingly sympathetic towards Heathcliff; see e.g. J. Twitchell, 'Heathcliff as Vampire', *Southern Humanities Review*, 11 (1977), 355–62. The best-known attempt to rehabilitate Heathcliff at Nelly Dean's expense is J. Hafsley's 'The Villain in *Wuthering Heights*', *Nineteenth-Century Fiction*, 13 (Dec. 1958), 199–215.

5. Like Edgar Linton, and many Brontë critics, I distinguish between mother and daughter by calling the elder 'Catherine' and the younger 'Cathy'.

6. Nelly to Lockwood, vol. 1, ch. viii, p. 65 in the World's Classics edition of *Wuthering Heights*, ed. I. Jack (Oxford, 1981); all subsequent references to the text of *Wuthering Heights* are to this edition.

7. Vol. 1, ch. v, p. 41.

8. See vol. 1, ch. x, p. 91. The only person who really likes Catherine is her sister-in-law Isabella, whose parents died of Catherine's febrile illness and whose own life is subsequently ruined, partly at Catherine's malicious instigation.

9. 'The Incest Theme in *Wuthering Heights*', *Nineteenth-Century Fiction*, 14 (June 1959), 80–3.

10. First printed in *Early Victorian Novelists* in 1935 and reprinted, in excerpts, in several volumes of *Wuthering Heights* criticism, including Allott's *Casebook* and the Norton Critical Edition of the novel.

11. Vol. 1, ch. v, p. 40.

12. Vol. 1, ch. viii, p. 66.

LISA WANG ON SPIRITUALITY IN *WUTHERING HEIGHTS*

The poetry examined thus far has depicted the role of the Spirit as life-giving wind, as comforter and advocate, and as *charism*, most significantly in relation to the kind of numinous religious experience involved in the poet's epiphanic apprehension of the divine nature. But the supreme value attached to this experience is most clearly articulated in Emily Brontë's penultimate surviving poem, 'No coward soul is mine' (1846).[34] The first half of this poem is a celebration of the power of the poet's 'Faith' in granting the ability to 'see Heaven's glories' while at the same time 'arming . . . from Fear'.[35] Echoing the words of Christ, 'abide in Me and I in you' (Jn 15:4), of Paul, 'the Spirit of God dwelleth in you' (I Co 3:16), and of John, 'God dwelleth in us' (I Jn 4:12), the poet declares:[36]

> O God within my breast
> Almighty ever-present Deity
> Life, that in me hast rest
> As I Undying Life, have power in Thee. (5–8)

The poet's expression of confidence in this mutual inter-relationship, with God resting in the poet and (s)he concomitantly drawing on God's power, appropriates the

73

biblical topos of the indwelling of the Holy Spirit in the believer: 'Hereby we know that we dwell in him, and he in us, because he hath given us of his Spirit' (I Jn 4:13). The Spirit thus takes on a central role in the believer's experience of God. It is no surprise, then, that in the second half of the poem the poet's understanding of the divine nature focuses on the figure of the Spirit:

> With wide-embracing love
> Thy spirit animates eternal years
> Pervades and broods above,
> Changes, sustains, dissolves, creates and rears. (17–20)

As in the earlier poems, the idea of the Spirit's creative or life-giving power is expressed using biblical imagery of 'the Spirit of God' as it 'moved on the face of the waters' (Ge 1:2), and of 'the Spirit descending from heaven like a dove' (Jn 2:32).[37] Similarly, the final lines of the poem make use of the idea of the Holy Spirit as the breath of God: 'Thou art Being and Breath / And what Thou art may never be destroyed.' What is articulated in this poem, then, through the use of such biblical tropes and topoi, is a confident belief in God's all-pervasive, life-giving Spirit; and what is celebrated (at the expense of the 'vain' and 'worthless' creeds which are the formal expressions of such belief) is the empowering experience of a direct and visceral relationship with such a Deity. These are themes that will play an important role in the study of the religious discourse in *Wuthering Heights*.

We have seen how, in Emily Brontë's poetry, biblical tropes and topoi relating to the Spirit inform the poet's depiction of the believer's experience of and relationship to the divine nature. In *Wuthering Heights*, the same concerns are present but without the linguistic constructions which make the theological framework so apparent in the poetry. Nevertheless, having considered the way in which these issues are approached in the poetry, it is possible to see more clearly their role in the novel's depiction of the relationship between Cathy and Heathcliff; in its treatment of the idea of transgression, and in the closing of the narrative.

On being pressed by Nelly to justify her engagement to Edgar Linton, Cathy attempts to describe the nature of her relationship with Heathcliff:

> there is, or should be, an existence of yours beyond you. What were the use of my creation if I were entirely contained here? . . . If all else perished, and *he* remained, I should still continue to be; and, if all else remained, and he were annihilated, the Universe would turn to a mighty stranger. I should not seem a part of it. . . . Nelly, I *am* Heathcliff—he's always, always in my mind—not as a pleasure, any more than I am always a pleasure to myself—but as my own being.[38]

Cathy insists that her 'being' is so closely linked to Heathcliff's that her very existence is somehow dependent on his. (Indeed, Heathcliff seems to echo this idea when he raves to the departed Cathy, '*do* not leave me in this abyss, where I cannot find you! Oh, God! it is unutterable! I *cannot* live without my life! I *cannot* live without my soul!' (204).) What is significant about this formula of inter-relationship is that it utilises the same language that the speaker of Emily Brontë's poem 'No coward soul is mine' (1846) uses to describe God:

> Though Earth and moon were gone
> And suns and universes ceased to be
> And thou wert left alone
> Every existence would exist in thee. (21–4)

This similarity suggests that the novel's depiction of the relationship between Cathy and Heathcliff draws on the understanding, presented in the poem, of the relationship between God and the believer. Since, as we have seen, the poem uses biblical topoi of the indwelling of the Holy Spirit to describe the inter-existential relationship of the believer to God, it may be said that Cathy's use of a similar paradigm to describe her love for Heathcliff suggests that she 'dwells' in him in a similar way that the Spirit does the believer. (In this context Heathcliff's statement that 'existence, after losing her, would be hell' (182) may be seen to echo the theological notion that hell is the eternal deprivation of God's presence.)

However, the novel, though it does seem to endorse the supreme value of some kind of transcendental experience of relational existence, cannot be said to celebrate such a relationship in the way that the poem does, for Cathy and Heathcliff are tormented by the problematic nature of their love. The indications of profound conflict in Heathcliff and Cathy's supposed unity seem to suggest that the spiritual paradigm outlined in 'No coward soul' cannot be successfully applied to personal relationships, if only because a finite, imperfect being cannot perform the work of an infinite, perfect being. This becomes apparent as Cathy finds herself drawn to Edgar Linton. Initially, Cathy believes that since her existence is 'contained' in Heathcliff's, and his in hers, he 'comprehends in his person' her own 'feelings to Edgar' (101). But this expectation proves to be unfounded, with disastrous results. However much both Cathy and Heathcliff desire to be ontologically one, they find themselves at odds, tormented nearly until the very moment of her death by resentments, regrets, and recriminations:

'You have killed me . . . I care nothing for your sufferings. Why shouldn't you suffer?' . . .
'Don't torture me . . . You know you lie . . . how cruel you've been—cruel and false. . . . I have not one word of comfort—you deserve this.' . . .
'Let me alone. Let me alone . . . If I've done wrong, I'm dying for it. It is enough! You left me too; but . . . I forgive you. Forgive me!' . . .
'How can I?' (195–8)

and so on. Even after Cathy's death, indeed for the remainder of his life, Heathcliff's torment continues, as he goes on seeking something which he cannot quite find, demanding something which she cannot quite give: 'I could *almost* see her, and yet I *could* not! I ought to have sweat blood then, from the anguish of my yearning, from the fervour of my supplications to have but one glimpse! I had not one' (350–1). Yet despite this torture, he persists in his desire, saying: 'I have a single wish, and my whole being and faculties are yearning to attain it. . . . it has devoured my existence' (395). In the end, ceasing to eat and feverish with anguish, Heathcliff follows his desire down the path to his own destruction in much the same way Cathy did eighteen years before.

This question of the consequences of the love between Cathy and Heathcliff raises the issue of the larger significance of their relationship, its place in the novel as a whole. In this context it is useful to regard the matter in terms of transgression, that is, the overstepping of boundaries. The everyday boundaries and distinctions which help us to define and shape our understanding of the world are repeatedly broken down and blurred in *Wuthering Heights*, creating a constant state of fluctuation which is profoundly unsettling to the reader, and which calls into question conventional notions of reality.

Notes

34. See Hatfield, pp. 243–4.

35. Cf. Paul's description 'of the whole armour of God' which includes 'above all . . . the shield of faith' (Eph 6:11, 16).

36. See also John 14:17, 'the Spirit . . . dwelleth with you, and shall be in you': I Corinthians 6:19, 'your body is the temple of the Holy Ghost which is in you'.

37. See also Job 26:12–13 and Psalm 104:30. The image of the Holy Spirit as dove is common not only in Christian poetry but also in hymns such as Charles Wesley's well-known 'Come, Holy Ghost, our hearts inspire': 'Expand thy wings, celestial Dove, / Brood o'er our nature's night, / On our disordered spirits move, / And let there now be light.'

38. E. Brontë, *Wuthering Heights*, H. Marsden and I. Jack (eds), (Oxford: Clarendon Press, 1976) pp. 101–2. All quotations from *Wuthering Heights* are taken from this edition. Subsequent page references to the novel are given parenthetically in the text.

Works by Emily Brontë

Novel Editions

Wuthering Heights, as Ellis Bell (2 volumes, London: T.C. Newby, 1847; 1 volume, Boston: Coolidge & Wiley, 1848).

Wuthering Heights: An Authoritative Text, Backgrounds, Criticism. Edited by William M. Sale, Jr. and Richard J. Dunn. New York: Norton, 1990.

Wuthering Heights: Complete, Authoritative Text with Biographical and Historical Contexts, Critical History, and Essays from Five Contemporary Critical Perspectives. Edited by Linda H. Peterson. Boston: Bedford Books of St. Martin's Press, 1992.

Wuthering Heights. Edited by Ian R. Jack; with an introduction and notes by Patsy Stoneman. New York: Oxford University Press, 1998.

Wuthering Heights: Complete Text with Introduction, Contexts, and Critical Essays. Edited by Diane Long Hoeveler. Boston: Houghton Mifflin, 2002.

Poetry

Poems by Currer, Ellis, and Acton Bell, by Charlotte, Emily and Anne Brontë. London: Aylott & Jones, 1946; Philadelphia: Lea & Blanchard, 1948.

Collections

The Life and Works of Charlotte Brontë and Her Sisters. Edited by Shorter. New York: Holder & Stoughton, 1908; London: Hodder & Stoughton, 1910.

The Complete Poems of Emily Jane Brontë. Edited by Shorter. New York: Hodder & Stoughton, 1908; London: Hodder & Stoughton, 1910.

The Shakespeare Head Brontë. Edited by T.J. Wise and J.A. Symington, 19 volumes. Oxford: Blackwell, 1931–1938.

The Clarendon Edition of the Novels of the Brontës, Edited by I.R. Jack, 3 volumes. Oxford: Clarendon Press, 1969.

Annotated Bibliography

Gilbert, Sandra M. and Susan Gubar. "Looking Oppositely: Emily Brontë's Bible of Hell." *The Madwoman in the Attic: The Woman Writer and the Nineteenth-Century Literary Imagination.* New Haven, CT: Yale Nota Bene (2000): 248–308.

Gilbert and Gubar's essay is concerned with the wide range of literary influences on Emily Brontë. Beginning with a comparison of *Wuthering Heights* and *Frankenstein*, they discuss certain common themes to be found in these two highly enigmatic novels, such as the fate of subordinate female characters and a dependence on "evidentiary narratives." Milton's *Paradise Lost* is identified as the subtext for Emily Brontë's exploration of the theme of the pariah. "Given the metaphysical nature of *Wuthering Heights*, Catherine's definition of herself as 'an exile and outcast' inevitably suggests those trail-blazing exiles Adam, Eve, and Satan." Following their identification of this subtext, Gilbert and Gubar point out many other important allusions, including Blake's *Songs of Innocence*, Shakespeare's *King Lear*, and Jane Austen's *Northanger Abbey*.

Homans, Margaret. "Emily Brontë." *Women Writers and Poetic Identity: Dorothy Wordsworth, Emily Brontë, and Emily Dickinson.* Princeton, NJ: Princeton University Press (1980): 104–161.

Homans focuses on the loss of individual identity, citing the numerous transferences and dispersions that form a pervasive theme throughout *Wuthering Heights*. Homans maintains that self-alienation accounts for the death wish in the novel, a drive that serves a compensatory function and that explains Heathcliff's anticipation of death as the means to reunite him with Cathy, a time when they will "be lost in one repose."

Jacobs, Carol. "*Wuthering Heights*: At the Threshold of Interpretation." *Boundary II* vol. 7, no. 3 (Spring 1979): 49–62.

Focusing on the metaphor of the doorway in the first three chapters, Jacobs maintains that Lockwood's entry and subsequent banishment from both the fictional realm of Wuthering Heights and as narrator of the events marks his exile from the text of the novel. Jacobs further suggests that as a result of his exclusion from the "text" of *Wuthering Heights*, Lockwood is able to arrive at an understanding of the novel as a fiction upon a fiction. In a series of dreams which function as the medium between text and reality, Lockwood arrives a the heart of this irrational world only to find himself enclosed in a space laden with a variety dusty books, diaries and sermons. "*Wuthering Heights* is an annunciation of excommunication, both a fabrication in language of the real world—of that which is outside language (excommunication)—and then again an expulsion of the heretic from its own textuality."

Kiely, Robert. "*Wuthering Heights*: Emily Brontë, 1847." *The Romantic Novel in England*. Cambridge, MA: Harvard University Press (1972): 233–251.

Kiely discusses *Wuthering Heights* as a radical novel within the English tradition and praises Brontë for having created a narrative with no overt literary allusions though acknowledging that she has assuredly drawn on predecessors. With respect to the function of Nelly Dean as a narrator, Kiely sees her as the medium through which the extreme and opposing perspectives of Lockwood and Heathcliff are mediated, for neither one would be able to tell the story "without focusing almost exclusively on himself." Ultimately, Kiely maintains that *Wuthering Heights* is composed of a series of transformations whereby new situations and characters are synthesized, yet the novel remains a text in which the true nature of the relationship between Catherine and Heathcliff is never disclosed, for it is beyond the scope of reason.

Knoepflmacher, U.C. "*Wuthering Heights*: A Tragicomic Romance." From *Laughter & Despair: Readings in Ten Novels of the Victorian Era*. Berkeley: University of California Press (1971): 84–108.

Knoepflmacher discusses Emily Brontë's talent for blending humor with melodrama. Focusing on Lockwood's characterization as an urbane man, "a refugee from civilized society," Knoepflmacher maintains that he functions as the unreliable guide whose refined manners and comic perspective prove erroneous and full of misjudgments from the outset. Knoepflmacher concludes that *Wuthering Heights* consistently vacillates between the comic and the tragic only to be resolved vis-à-vis a new comic mode, namely the "quasi-Christian" love story of Cathy and Hareton, which remains, nevertheless, a diminutive version of the relationship between Catherine and Heathcliff.

Leavis, Q.D. "A Fresh Approach to 'Wuthering Heights.'" *Lectures in America* by F.R. Leavis and Q.D. Leavis. London: Chatto & Windus (1969): 83–152.

Identifying a wide range of English, American, and continental literary influences, as well as ballads, Q.D. Leavis discusses the way Emily Brontë draws from a rich and varied literary tradition and argues that *Wuthering Heights* is a novel of penetrating psychological insight. Leavis further maintains that *Wuthering Heights* also responds to the Romantic theme of childhood struggling against society, as well as the plight of border-farmers who fought to survive the wild and desolate moors. "*Wuthering Heights* thus became a responsible piece of work, and the writer thought herself into the positions, outlooks, sufferings and tragedies of the actors in these typical events as an *artist*."

Miller, J. Hillis. "Emily Brontë." *The Disappearance of God: Five Nineteenth-Century Writers*. Cambridge, MA: The Belknap Press of Harvard University Press (1963): 157–211.

J. Hillis Miller's essay discusses *Wuthering Heights* in the context of Brontë's visionary poetry and maintains that *Wuthering Heights*, which marked her communication with an anonymous reading public, represents a betrayal of the personal world of her poems. In a realm in which neighbor is set against neighbor, Miller states that animals become the medium through which the individual characters' spirituality is measured. "The characters in *Wuthering Heights* have returned to an animal state. Such a return is reached only through the transgression of all human law." Miller concludes that though the society of Wuthering Heights is restored to a benign status, spiritual restoration remains incomplete.

Oates, Joyce Carol. "The Magnanimity of *Wuthering Heights*." *Critical Inquiry*, vol. 9, no. 2 (December 1982): 435–449.

Lauding *Wuthering Heights* as a masterpiece of fiction incorporating both gothic and Romantic elements, Oates maintains that Emily Brontë succeeds in challenging the assumptions of both of these literary traditions in her presentation of two opposing yet intertwined tales at the same time. In response to the Romantic valorization of childhood, *Wuthering Heights* offers a nightmarish presentation of childhood (and the cruelty and betrayal of which children are capable) while simultaneously offering a counterbalancing narrative of growth, maturity, and accommodation to the material world. "It is this fidelity to the observed physical world, and Brontë's own inward applause, that makes the metamorphosis of the dark tale into its opposite so plausible, as well as so ceremonially appropriate."

Paris, Bernard. "*Wuthering Heights*." *Imagined Human Beings: A Psychological Approach to Character and Conflict in Literature*." New York: New York University Press (1997): 240–261.

Arguing that Heathcliff's character is entirely credible in human terms—rather than serving a symbolic function, as some critics have maintained—Paris focuses on his childhood as the motivation for his cruel nature. Paris makes the case that *Wuthering Heights* is ultimately about human attachments and suffering, "merger and separation," and that Emily Brontë demonstrates a keen psychological insight in the display of extreme emotions and behavior. Ultimately, Paris maintains that the novel proffers a solution in which moderation is restored in the marriage of the second Catherine to Hareton Earnshaw. "The members of the second generation are better, in part at least, because they have been better treated. The marriage of Hareton and Cathy represents the triumph of love and forgiveness over hatred and revenge. . . ."

Sonstroem, David. "*Wuthering Heights* and the Limits of Vision. *PMLA* vol. 86, no. 1 (January 1971): 51–62.

David Sonstroem discusses *Wuthering Heights* as an amalgam of disparate and myopic points of view in conflict with one another due to the characters' limitations. He argues that this shortsightedness is thematized in the many instances in which people are invalidated and expectations proved erroneous. Sonstroem concludes that Emily Brontë is depicting a Victorian state of mind that is suffering in its refusal to confront its own preconceived notions and intolerances—political, social, religious, or otherwise—and therefore remains fragmented beyond comprehension. Furthermore, he asserts that the author can be found at the heart of her narrative. "The stumbling shortsightedness she presents in her characters and induces in her readers is in fact her own experience of the world and the burden of her message."

Stanford, Derek, and Muriel Spark. "'*Wuthering Heights*': Plot and Players." *Emily Brontë: Her Life and Work*. London: Peter Owen (1953): 238–258.

Beginning his character analysis with an extended discussion of Heathcliff's dramatic manner of speaking, which he maintains is comparable to that of the Byronic hero, Stanford contrasts Heathcliff to the minor figures of Joseph and Nelly Dean, who he describes as "static" personalities, in that neither one changes his or her manner of speaking or behavior. Turning his analysis to Catherine, Stanford finds her to be the most original and fully developed character within the novel, a presence that overshadows Heathcliff in terms of a unique personality. Stanford maintains that she is comparable to Shakespeare's Katharina. "Catherine, it is true, has a prototype in literature. . . . None the less, it is interesting to notice that Emily's heroine bears the same name as Shakespeare's Katharina, in *The Taming of the Shrew*. But Emily's shrew is a tragic one; and Cathy (her daughter who—in some ways—completes her mother's emotional intention) is not overcome by ring-master tactics, but by Hareton's independent nature, thawing out into co-operation and affection."

Steinitz, Rebecca. "Diaries and Displacement in *Wuthering Heights*." *Studies in the Novel*, vol. 32, no. 4 (Winter 2000): 407–419.

Stressing the importance of immediacy and the first-person accounts of events from the opening lines of *Wuthering Heights*, which begins with Lockwood's journal entry recording his return from Wuthering Heights, Steinitz argues that the diary at first functions as a framing device until the third chapter in which it becomes a material instrument for cataloguing the novels passionate and tumultuous history. Steinitz maintains that the significance of the diary, having heretofore been subsumed by such other critical rubrics of texts within texts, is essential to understanding the text and the particularity to which it refers. "Indeed, despite their many differences of status, both Catherine and Lockwood . . . use their diaries to deal precisely with their senses of displacement. . . . [T]he diary itself becomes the proverbial place of one's own, but its very status as such reveals how, psychologically, textually, and materially, one's own place can never be secured."

Stoneman, Patsy. "Catherine Earnshaw's Journey to Her Home Among the Dead: Fresh Thoughts on *Wuthering Heights* and 'Epipsychidion.'" *The Review of English Studies*, vol. 47, no. 188 (November 1996): 521–533.

Citing the English Romantic poets as the contemporaries of Brontë's youth, Stoneman argues that Percy Bysshe Shelley's poem "Epipsychidion," the title and subject matter being representative of a transcendent concept of "Romantic love" in which two souls unite rather than traditional notions of romantic love as courtship and marriage, is particularly relevant to an understanding of *Wuthering Heights*. Stoneman states that though the "Romantic love" exemplified in Shelley's poem is problematic for most readers, it is the only means for understanding Catherine's otherwise "preposterous" assumptions, such as her joy that Heathcliff returns only to discover her marriage to Edgar. "No sense of tragic irony seems to enter into her consciousness, nor any foreboding of difficulties."

Thormählen, Marianne. "The Lunatic and the Devil's Disciple: The 'Lovers' in *Wuthering Heights.*" *The Review of English Studies*, vol. 48, no. 190 (May 1997): 183–197.

Thormählen discusses the doomed nature of the love relationship between Catherine and Heathcliff by focusing on the monstrous aspects of their individual characterizations. Describing Catherine's outrageous behavior as "pathologically egotistical," Thormählen contends that Catherine's preoccupation with herself is something beyond adolescent self-absorption, citing such evidence as her complete identification with Heathcliff, so that he becomes merely an extension of herself, "an integral part of her egomania." With respect to Heathcliff, Thormählen maintains that his character is aligned with the devil from the start. This is suggested by his first appearance at Wuthering Heights, a "dark" child who brings disruption to the household, to his rapid transformation into an educated man of means, attended by such words as "devil" and "diabolical," implying some malevolent intervention on his behalf.

Wang, Lisa. "The Holy Spirit in Emily Brontë's *Wuthering Heights* and Poetry." *Literature & Theology*, vol. 14, no. 2 (June 2000): 160–173.

Analyzing *Wuthering Heights* in terms of Emily Brontë's education and the biblical tropes in her poetry and citing the scarcity of biblical allusions in the novel, Wang maintains that *Wuthering Heights* privileges fundamental religious experience over specific doctrinal issues. She argues that the spirituality of *Wuthering Heights* presents a qualitative difference from Brontë's poetry in that there is no absolute resolution in the novel. Using the symbolism of the wind, which remains in a state of flux at the novel's end, Wang concludes that the reader is not at all assured a world of tranquility. "This is the final image of *Wuthering Heights*, not an image of resolution or peace, nor of violence or despair, but of a universe whose only element of constancy is its everchangingness."

Watson, Melvin R. "Tempest in the Soul: The Theme and Structure of *Wuthering Heights.*" *Nineteenth-Century Fiction*, vol. 4, no. 2 (September 1949): 87–100.

A recognized classic in *Wuthering Heights* criticism, Watson's essay discusses the novel as a psychological study of an enigmatic man torn between the two opposing passions of love and hate, the narrative structure of which resembles the five-act tragedy of Elizabethan drama. Watson contends that Heathcliff, the dominant personality to which all other characters are subordinate, is an embittered soul capable of transformation given time and more auspicious circumstances and that, consequently, *Wuthering Heights* achieves a felicitous conclusion in the second-generation love story of young Cathy and Hareton. "The love which develops out of and in spite of the hate which surrounds them—but develops as that hate is subsiding—provides the calm and symbolic ending of the book."

Woodring, Carl. "The Narrators of *Wuthering Heights.*" *Nineteenth-Century Fiction*, vol. 11, no. 4 (March 1957): 298–305.

Woodring begins with a discussion of the double narrative convention of Lockwood and Nelly Dean as dual narrators: the stranger who participates in the reader's amazement and the intimate who bears witness to the strange history of Wuthering Heights, respectively. Having made this fundamental distinction, Woodring further elucidates the differences in their characters and the consequential viewpoints that they provide. Lockwood, the "educated diarist from the city," speaks in prose, while Nelly Dean employs the simple language of a servant and inhabitant of the moors, though serving a highly elaborate function throughout the novel. "Attentive witness, narrator, and elucidator of past events, Mrs. (that is, Miss) Dean not only plays an active role economically designed, but also commands interest as a personality. . . ."

Contributors

Harold Bloom is Sterling Professor of the Humanities at Yale University. He is the author of 30 books, including *Shelley's Mythmaking*, *The Visionary Company*, *Blake's Apocalypse*, *Yeats*, *A Map of Misreading*, *Kabbalah and Criticism*, *Agon: Toward a Theory of Revisionism*, *The American Religion*, *The Western Canon*, and *Omens of Millennium: The Gnosis of Angels, Dreams, and Resurrection*. *The Anxiety of Influence* sets forth Professor Bloom's provocative theory of the literary relationships between the great writers and their predecessors. His most recent books include *Shakespeare: The Invention of the Human*, a 1998 National Book Award finalist, *How to Read and Why*, *Genius: A Mosaic of One Hundred Exemplary Creative Minds*, *Hamlet: Poem Unlimited*, *Where Shall Wisdom Be Found?*, and *Jesus and Yahweh: The Names Divine*. In 1999, Professor Bloom received the prestigious American Academy of Arts and Letters Gold Medal for Criticism. He has also received the International Prize of Catalonia, the Alfonso Reyes Prize of Mexico, and the Hans Christian Andersen Bicentennial Prize of Denmark.

Melvin R. Watson is professor emeritus of English and comparative literature at Chapman University in California. He is the author of *Magazine Serials and the Essay Tradition, 1746–1820* (1956), "The Redemption of *Peter Bell*" (1964), and "*Wuthering Heights* and the Critics" (1949).

Muriel Spark (1918–2006) was one of the most important Scottish writers of the late twentieth century. In addition to her literary criticism and essays, she wrote critical biographies, poetry, and novels, most notably *The Prime of Miss Jean Brodie*.

Derek Stanford has been a professor of writing and literature at the University of Chester. He is the author of *Poets of the 'Nineties'* (1965), *Dylan Thomas: A Literary Study* (1954), and *Inside the Forties: Literary Memoirs, 1937–1957* (1977).

J. Hillis Miller has been a professor of English and comparative literature at the University of California, Irvine. He is the author of *Versions of Pygmalion* (1990), *Ariadne's Thread: Story Lines* (1992) and *Reading Narrative* (1998).

Q.D. Leavis (1906–1981) was an English literary critic and essayist. She was the author of *Fiction and the Reading Public* (1932), *Dickens the Novelist* (1970), and several volumes of collected essays titled *The Englishness of the English Novel* (1983), *The American Novel and Reflections on the European Novel* (1985), and *The Novel of Religious Controversy* (1989).

U.C. Knoepflmacher has been a professor of English at Princeton University. He is the author of *Ventures into Childland: Victorians, Fairy Tales, and Femininity* (1998), *Emily Brontë: Wuthering Heights* (1989), and *Religious Humanism and the Victorian Novel* (1965).

Carol Jacobs has been Birgit Baldwin Professor of Comparative Literature at Yale University. She is the author of *In the Language of Walter Benjamin* (1999), *Uncontainable Romanticism: Shelley, Brontë, Kleist* (1989), and *The Dissimulating Harmony: The Image of Interpretation in Nietzsche, Rilke, Artaud, and Benjamin* (1978).

Sandra M. Gilbert has been professor of English at the University of California, Davis. Along with Susan Gubar, she published *Madwoman in the Attic: The Woman Writer and the Nineteenth-Century Literary Imagination* in 1979, a finalist for both the Pulitzer Prize and the National Book Critics Circle Award. Gilbert is the author of a prose memoir, *Wrongful Death: A Medical Tragedy*, and many books of poetry, including *Ghost Volcano, Inventions of Farewell: A Book of Elegies*, and *Kissing the Bread: New and Selected Poems*.

Susan Gubar has been Distinguished Professor of English and women's studies at Indiana University. Along with Sandra M. Gilbert, she published *The Madwoman in the Attic: The Woman*

Writer and the Nineteenth-Century Literary Imagination. Gilbert and Gubar also coauthored *No Man's Land: The Place of the Woman Writer in the Twentieth Century; The War of the Words, Sexchanges,* and *Letters from the Front.* Gubar is the author of *Racechanges: White Skin, Black Face in American Culture* and the editor of *Critical Condition: Feminism at the Turn of the Century.*

Patsy Stoneman has been a reader in English at the University of Hull. She is the author of *Brontë Transformations: The Cultural Dissemination of Jane Eyre and Wuthering Heights* (1996) and *Elizabeth Gaskell* (1987) and editor of *Jane Eyre on Stage, 1848–1898: An Illustrated Edition of Eight Plays with Contextual Notes* (2007).

Bernard J. Paris has taught at Lehigh University, Michigan State, and the University of Florida, where he is emeritus professor of English and former director of the Institute for Psychological Study of the Arts. He is the author of *Character as a Subversive Force in Shakespeare: The History and Roman Plays* (1991) *A Psychological Approach to Fiction: Studies in Thackeray, Stendhal, George Eliot, Dostoevsky, and Conrad* (1974), and *Experiments in Life: George Eliot's Quest for Values* (1965).

Marianne Thormählen has been professor of English literature, Lund University, Sweden. She is the author of *The Brontës and Education* (2007), *The Brontës and Religion* (1999), and *Rochester: The Poems in Context* (1993).

Lisa Wang is the author of "Unveiling the Hidden God of Charlotte Brontë's 'Villette'" (2001).

Acknowledgments

Melvin R. Watson, from "Tempest in the Soul: The Theme and Structure of 'Wuthering Heights' *Nineteenth-Century Fiction*, vol. 4, no. 2 (September 1949), pp. 87–100. © University of California Press. Reprinted with permission.

Muriel Spark and Derek Stanford, from *Emily Bronte: Her Life and Work*, pp. 248–253. London: Peter Owen Limited, 1953. Reprinted with permission.

J. Hillis Miller, Reprinted by permission of the publisher from *The Disappearance of God: Five Nineteenth-Century Writers* by J. Hillis Miller, pp. 165-168, Cambridge, Mass.: The Belknap Press of Harvard University Press, Copyright © 1963, 1975 by the President and Fellows of Harvard College.

Q.D. Leavis, from *Lectures in America* by F.R. Leavis and Q.D. Leavis, published by Chatto & Windus. Reprinted by permission of The Random House Group Ltd.

U.C. Knoepflmacher, from "*Wuthering Heights:* A Tragicomic Romance" from *Laughter & Despair: Readings in Ten Novels of the Victorian Era*, pp. 87–89, 107–108. © 1971 by the Regents of the University of California. Reprinted with permission.

Carol Jacobs, from "*Wuthering Heights:* At the Threshold of Interpretation" from *boundary 2*, vol. 7, no. 3, Revisions of the Anglo-American Tradition: Part 2 (Spring 1979), pp. 50–53. © Duke University Press.

Sandra M. Gilbert and Susan Gubar, The Madwoman in the Attic: The Woman Writer and the Nineteenth-Century Literary Imagination, Second Edition, pp. 252–255. New Haven: Yale University Press, 1979. © 1984 by Sandra M. Gilbert and Susan Gubar.

Patsy Stoneman, from "Catherine Earnshaw's Journey to Her Home among the Dead: Fresh Thoughts on *Wuthering Heights* and 'Epipsychidion,'" from *The Review of English Studies*, new series, vol. 47, no. 188 (November 1996), pp. 523–526. Reprinted by permission of Oxford University Press.

Bernard J. Paris, from *Imagined Human Beings: A Psychological Approach to Character and Conflict in Literature*, pp. 241–244. New York: New York University Press, 1997. © 1997 New York University.

Marianne Thormählen, from "The Lunatic and the Devil's Disciple: The 'Lovers' in *Wuthering Heights*," from *The Review of English Studies*, new series, vol. 48, no. 190 (May 1997), pp. 183–186. Reprinted by permission of Oxford University Press.

Lisa Wang, from "The Holy Spirit in Emily Brontë's *Wuthering Heights* and Poetry," from *Literature & Theology, vol. 14, no. 2 (June 2000) pp. 165*–168, 172–173. Reprinted by permission of Oxford University Press.

Index

Characters in literary works are indexed by first name (if any), followed by the name of the work in parentheses.

Gloucester County
Library System